IN OUR HANDS

A HISTORY OF
COMMUNITY BUSINESS

by
Steve Wyler

IN OUR HANDS

A HISTORY OF COMMUNITY BUSINESS

"Over the centuries communities have used business to tackle problems they faced. The community businesses we've worked with recently are harnessing the same combination of civic action and entrepreneurialism to create new models for 21st Century challenges. This book offers insight and inspiration to those wanting to make a difference today."

- Matthew Taylor, Chief Executive, RSA

"Learning how to make community business work is something where we need history to tell us what works and what doesn't. I can think of nobody more capable of sharing insights on this than Steve Wyler. His clear, thoughtful and inspiring book should help many who struggle to make local and beneficial businesses flourish."

- Professor Anne Power, London School of Economics

"This readable book reminds all of us engaged in civil society that we truly stand on the shoulders of giants. In tracing our history in such an engaging and readable way, Steve Wyler allows us to rethink our future, and in particular to understand the power of mutual support and solidarity in difficult times."

- Julia Unwin, Chair, Independent Inquiry into the Future of Civil Society

Published in 2017 by CoVi Productions.
CoVi Productions is a trading name of Common Vision UK, a company limited by guarantee registered in England and Wales, number 08837291.

ISBN 978-1-5272-1335-7

See further information and resources at
www.historyofcommunitybusiness.co.uk

Contents

Part 4

Part 5

Part 6

Preface

A spirit of community business is abroad...

We live at a time when communities across the UK face an uncertain and precarious future.

Whoever we are and wherever we live we need not go far to see for ourselves how the dismantling of public services, enduring social problems, and changing patterns of work have cast a shadow over many lives and have brought blight to many places. As we look around we can see that the local pub, the local shop, the local library, those institutions which have been at the heart of neighbourhood life for so many generations, are struggling for survival, and often failing in that struggle.

And yet this is not the whole story.

A spirit of community business is abroad, and wherever it arrives, it breathes fresh life into neighbourhoods, awakening and invigorating, bringing cherished facilities back to life and inspiring new ones, and generating new confidence, pride and hopefulness.

In inner city neighbourhoods and in run-down estates, in old industrial towns and in villages which have been left behind, in the very places where the economy is most broken and the people have been written off most often, it seems to be community business which is stepping forward with the best solutions.

Home-grown solutions, emerging from lived experience and deep local knowledge. Solutions fuelled by a defiant and entrepreneurial never-say-die and yes-we-can spirit. Solutions born from solidarity, from a conscious decision of people in a community to stand together, to support each other, to take back control.

A lot of this feels exciting and new. A community taking over land so that it can build affordable housing. A community share issue which raises hundreds of thousands of pounds from local residents. A community running public services, instead of the local council, and doing it better. A community business up against private competition, and beating all-comers hands down.

But is any of this really new? Of course not. Naturally all community businesses will feel that they are pioneers, and always in some sense they are. Usually their supporters and funders and the policy makers are happy to go along with the idea, because everyone likes to be seen to be an innovator, at the forefront of something distinctive, and leading the way.

But the truth is that as far as community business is concerned we are not starting at year zero. Far from it. For generation after generation, stretching back hundreds of years, people have harnessed the entrepreneurial instinct as a force for public good, not just for private benefit.

So what exactly is a community business? Today we might say that it is a business designed to make a long term positive difference for a community, controlled and run by local people for local people. Just like any other business it seeks to generate surpluses and build up assets. However, these are applied for the benefit of the community rather than for private gain. No one gets rich from a community business, but, if successful, everyone gains.

The phrase 'community business' is not the only way to describe such ventures. Community enterprise means very much the same thing and social enterprise is another term in widespread use, although one that doesn't necessarily imply a deep connection to a particular place.

But what's in a name? What matters most is what the community business is aiming to do, what it actually does, how it does it, and whether the community really is in control. One way to think about a community business is to see it as the meeting place of public, private and voluntary endeavour. Over the course of history, community businesses have taken many forms, but time and again they have demonstrated that it is indeed possible to combine civic responsibility with entrepreneurial instincts and harness them for the common good, and at the same time apply the simple but profound insight that the people within a community are a deep reservoir of skill and talent and shared support.

In the following pages we will follow the many-threaded and sometimes tangled story of community business.

One thread is mutual aid, which can be traced all the way back to the medieval guilds, and which emerges again in the friendly and benefit societies, and ultimately and most vigorously in the co-operative movement, where very large numbers of community businesses were set up and run by working people themselves.

Another thread is philanthropy, the impulse behind the trading ventures established by charitable or religious institutions, by benevolent industrialists, or by wealthy social reformers.

A third thread is social change, where community business was regarded as an integral and necessary feature of a world transformed by a radically new, more equitable, and truly liberating social order.

Many community businesses today display a combination of all these threads. Indeed the best hold them all in a creative tension, whereby mutual aid is supported and strengthened rather than stifled by philanthropy, and the urge to pioneer radically different models of social organisation provides an ever-present driving energy.

The history of community business has never followed an entirely simple path. It would be wrong to think that there was a clear moment when community business began, and that across all the succeeding generations there was continual and linear progress.

In truth, the story which is told in the following chapters, and which can also be found in the on-line resources which accompany this book, is less straightforward. The origins of community business turn out to be multiple and far-remote: as we shall see in the next section the precursors of community business can be traced back at least to the ancient Roman '*collegia*' and the '*gildonia*' of early medieval Europe, as well as to the later medieval craft guilds.

Over the succeeding centuries many different forms of community business emerged. Some were revolutionary in intent, while others were reformist or even conservative in purpose and practice. Some were determinedly secular and others were motivated by a religious impulse. Some were designed and led by impoverished working people, others by the wealthiest classes.

As we shall see, there have been many obstacles along the way and many false starts. Detours and distractions have always been part of the story of community business. And while many ideas and experiences were passed down from one generation to the next, a great deal was also lost, at least for a time. This is sometimes a stop-start history. The inventions of time-banking, and of raising finance through community shares, both of which attracted great interest in the early 19th century, were all but forgotten for 150 years, only to be re-invented all over again in the last two decades.

And yet, even if the path of community business has never been entirely straightforward or simple, community business as an idea and as a practice has endured and has grown. It seems to have flourished especially in times when it is most needed, when the alternatives were plainly just not good enough. And so, as we look around us today, it is perhaps no surprise to see the community business movement so vigorous, so full of hope, so much on the front foot.

PART ONE:
COMMUNITY BUSINESS
IN A FEUDAL SOCIETY

For many hundreds of years the story of community business was a story of local craftsman and traders, working first and foremost for their own benefit, but also and increasingly taking on responsibilities for their colleagues and for their wider community.

This was an age of rigid hierarchies, initially allowing little scope for social mobility. The Norman occupation of England had imposed a form of social organisation and property ownership dominated by a wealthy and powerful minority. The vast majority of the population lived a subsistence life. On the one hand they were in bondage to feudal lords who controlled most aspects of their lives. On the other they were required to pay tithes to the institutions of the church, which accumulated vast wealth.

But from the 12th century onwards the growth of towns and cities and flourishing trade created conditions for greater independence among tradesmen and craftsmen, who organised themselves into guilds for their own protection and self-interest. These guilds were primarily designed to prevent the encroachment of outsiders and keep the prices of the goods high, by establishing cartels and maintaining production standards. But the guilds were also local mutual aid societies, providing assistance for guild members in difficulty and their families.

Over time the guilds prospered, and many became wealthy in their own right. They extended their activities into many areas of civic and community life: they established policing and provided sanitation, they built market facilities, alms houses, schools, and hospitals, and they established charities for relief of the poor.

The guilds can be seen as a precursor of community business, a demonstration that community self-organisation and entrepreneurial activity could be a powerful combination for social improvement, and their example was never entirely forgotten by those who followed after.

In the 1500s the guilds lost much of their power. When Henry VIII broke away from Rome much of the property of the guilds was confiscated by the Crown, and in the reign of Elizabeth I the Statute of Artificers took away their responsibility for regulating apprenticeships.

This was followed by an increased role for the state and also for charities. But the need for mutual aid persisted. Over the following centuries the guilds were replaced by a rich variety of friendly societies: box clubs, societies of freemasons, Oddfellows clubs, and other types of benefit society.

These performed first and foremost a social insurance function, a way to make provision in case of sickness, occupational injury, and old age. They proliferated, becoming a widespread alternative to the charity model, run not by wealthy philanthropists but rather by the common people themselves. Over succeeding generations they built a culture of association and solidarity, which was to greatly influence the future development of community business.

Community confraternities

Mutual aid societies, operating in a local community, and established for social and economic benefit, were already in existence in Roman times, some 2,000 years ago.

These were the *collegia* which had flourished across the Roman empire. For the mass of common people, the plebians, life within the complex and highly centralised Roman system was hard, and Roman laws were harsh by any standard. The state was omnipresent, but provided little or no help for those who were sick or infirm. So the *collegia* were the means for sections of the population who had no civic power to organise themselves into associations in which they could stand together for their own protection and welfare. Even slaves could sometimes belong, and the *collegia* were able to serve a variety of purposes: burial societies, social clubs, trade associations, and religious cults, or a combination of these.

They even invented their own mythology. As related by Plutarch, the *collegia* claimed to be able to trace their foundation all the way back to Numa the second king of Rome, who, it was said, was responsible for organising eight artisan trades into colleges: musicians, goldsmiths, carpenters, dyers, shoemakers, tanners, braziers, and potters.

The *collegia* established meeting halls and these were sometimes known as the *'curia'*, in other words, the Senate Houses of the people. Fees and dues went into a common chest called the *'arca'*, and some portion of the funds collected may have been used for charitable purposes as well as for members' funeral expenses and communal meals. Most *collegia* enjoyed the support of a patron drawn from the higher classes, often a woman, who might contribute to the expenses of the group.

However, not everyone regarded them in a favourable light, particularly members of the elite who viewed the lower orders with deep suspicion and fear. The historian Suetonius wrote that they were 'in reality organisations for committing every sort of crime'. Occasionally suppressed, the *collegia* were generally permitted to operate by the senatorial classes, not least because they proved to be a good way of co-opting the wider population into the system of Roman rule.

When the Roman empire collapsed so did the *collegia*, but associative activity re-emerged in new forms. From the time of Charlemagne, *gildonia* appeared across Northern Europe. These were groups of citizens who came together within a parish for two main purposes: almsgiving and drunken feasts. In the year 852 Archbishop Hincmar of Reims approved the former and condemned the latter, banning the holding of guild banquets at which, according to him, priests and laymen entertained each other with 'idiotic tales', wore masks, and played obscene tricks.

In the early Islamic world artisan organisations such as the *warraqeen* (those who work with paper) became prominent trade associations, with paper makers, scribes, and booksellers promoting a culture of shared knowledge across the Muslim world. In Italy there were the *ministeria* of Lombardy, groups of artisans, boatmen, fishermen, and soap makers, bound together by collective obligations to the monarch: they were required to provide goods for the court, and in return enjoyed royal protection, and so members of the *ministeria* organised themselves to share tasks on an equitable basis.

In Anglo Saxon England a type of *gildonia* evolved which took on tasks of mutual protection and keeping the peace, as well as religious duties, and the first guildhalls were constructed for their members to meet. It seems that at this time it was believed that the duties of one guild member to another did not end at death, but rather continued and increased, linking the souls of the living and the dead into a perpetual confraternity.

The merchant and craft guilds which evolved in the twelfth century in England probably owed something to all these antecedents. These medieval guilds were driven first and foremost by self-interest: above all the need to keep the price of their goods high. And so their primary function was to prevent others coming in and undercutting their prices, and to prevent over-production. With members of the craft guilds operating small businesses and family workshops, they were protectionist and anti-competitive from the start, in effect a form of localised cartel. They had powers to regulate working conditions, to control who was admitted into the profession, and to limit working hours, for example by prohibiting guild work on the numerous Saints days.

Over time, the guilds found themselves engaged in activities for the collective good: they provided assistance for members and their families who fell on hard times; they took on apprentices and so trained the next generation; they introduced rules which prevented the sale of shoddy products which might undermine the reputation of the group; and eventually, as they became wealthy, their good works extended beyond their immediate membership, and they embarked on religious and civic projects of benefit to the wider community.

Guilds often placed great emphasis on their spiritual and religious functions, but they also engaged in extensive civic works which made a big impact on the society of their day. Grouped by trade the guilds controlled not only the local economy but also invested in the fabric of the neighbourhood, establishing market squares, schools, hospitals, and almshouses, building bridges and improving the roads, and sweeping and policing the streets. At first these facilities were intended to be for the benefit of guild members only, but over time they became amenities for the community as a whole.

And so the guilds led the way for urban self-determination. Previously towns and cities had grown around royal or ecclesiastical centres, castles, palaces and cathedrals, relying on the protection and patronage of these institutions and reflecting their power. But now towns and cities became something else as well: places with a core of civic amenities at their heart, produced through the combined wealth of local citizens, through trade.

It is evident that these early guilds provided a structure for commercial activity which contained a high degree of social organisation, in which the notion that profit should be used for social good was widely accepted. In some cities, the guilds also had considerable political influence. To this day the 110 London guilds (the 'livery companies') still control London's Square Mile: they make up the City Corporation and elect the Lord Mayor of London.

While men of course predominated, the guilds were not entirely closed to women. In many trades women played a significant part, as tanners, cordwainers, skinners, parchment makers, fishmongers, alewives (often alongside husbands who were bakers), hostellers, and weavers. While membership was barred to women in some guilds, that was not universally the case. It was not unknown, on the death of a Master Craftsman, for his wife to take over. For example in 1441, two years after the death of her husband, Isabella Nonhouse became a Master Weaver in York, and around the same time Margaret Soureby in York and Joan Hille in London operated foundries, employing many male apprentices.

Increasingly the medieval guilds were controlled by wealthy elites, seeking to preserve their own private interests, and exercising dominion over the public realm for their own purposes. But even so, they continued to invest significant amounts of their profits for social good, and so demonstrated the possibility of combining business methods and community benefit. Their example helped to inspire subsequent generations of reformers, radicals, and social revolutionaries.

From guilds to friendly societies

Across Europe the power of the guilds was weakened by the Protestant Reformation, and in England thousands of guilds were suppressed following the 1534 Act of Supremacy when Henry VIII broke from the Roman Catholic Church. Government agents were sent to seize guild property as well as any guild funds retained for religious purposes, and the guilds that survived were forced to pay large sums for the right to remain in operation.

A further blow came in 1563 when the Statute of Artificers transferred much of the authority previously exercised by the guilds to the newly forming English state: magistrates were given the power to set wages, to regulate apprenticeships, and to approve transfer from one employer to another, and at the same time certain superior trades were reserved for the sons and daughters of the propertied classes.

As the economic and political power of the guilds was diminished, so too was their ability to address social problems, which continued to grow at an alarming rate in Tudor Britain. Towards the end of the reign of Elizabeth I the situation had become so serious that finally action was taken on a national scale.

One solution adopted was an increase in taxation and state welfare. From the turn of the 17th century, welfare and other municipal services were regulated by national legislation and became a duty on the parish council to deliver, through the collection of local rates, and the first workhouses were established.

At the same time legislation was passed to encourage the growth of charities. The Statute of Elizabeth I in 1601 defined charitable purpose as 'the relief of aged, impotent, and poor people' as well as other purposes such as the repair of bridges, churches, and highways, the provision of schools and the education of orphans. In other words many of the activities where the guilds had played a significant role were now to be taken forward within a charity model. The new charity legislation was used by surviving guilds as well as religious institutions to establish charitable foundations, and increasingly by wealthy individuals from among the nobility, the growing merchant classes, and early industrialists, and a new system of organised philanthropy was inaugurated.

But although the guilds had taken a step back, and the state and charities had taken a step forward, the need for ordinary people to come together for mutual benefit did not diminish, and so new forms of association emerged. For example, box clubs would meet at public houses on a specified meeting day. These were convivial occasions, though usually well regulated: members would drink a specified amount of beer each time they met. They would contribute funds to a box with three locks, which would be looked after by the publican. Members in need might receive funds from the box for sickness or disability, burial expenses for the member or member's spouse, loss of property due to fire, imprisonment for debt, or, in the case of women, lying-in.

An early recorded example of this type of mutual aid was the Brotherly Meeting of the Masters and Workmen Printers, formed in London in about 1621. Another was the Friendly Benefit Society of Bethnal Green, formed in 1687. The Oddfellows started as clubs of this kind, meeting for social evenings at taverns, with songs, toasts, and collections for members in difficulty.

Box clubs, societies of freemasons, and other benefit societies, or 'friendly societies' as many of them came to be known, were seen by the authorities as a way of preventing destitution and curtailing the rising cost of parish relief. In 1793 an Act was passed 'for the encouragement and relief of friendly societies,' which authorised them to make 'proper and wholesome Rules not repugnant to the laws of the realm.'

This Act noted that 'the protection and encouragement of Friendly Societies … is likely to be attended with very beneficial effects by promoting the happiness of individuals and at the same time diminishing the public burdens.' As so often in the history of community business, regulation was used as a form of political control. The Act was introduced in the aftermath of the French Revolution, at a time when an anxious government saw the possibility of sedition in every gathering of working people, and no doubt one purpose of the Act was to regulate these societies with a firmer hand.

Nevertheless, by 1801 Sir Frederic Eden estimated that there were 7,200 friendly societies in England and Wales, with about 628,000 members. Burial clubs became particularly popular as they provided a means to avoid the dreaded 'pauper's funeral', and in the absence of universal old age pensions annuity societies and widow's funds also flourished, while deposit friendly societies performed the function of a savings bank.

Sometimes, especially in rural areas, persons of property and influence joined societies as honorary members and treasurers, or formed committees to regulate the friendly societies, and in such cases the club rules were usually drafted by the gentry. But this was not always the case, and increasingly the societies provided an opportunity for the 'respectable' lower orders, particularly in towns and cities, to gain experience of office holding and financial administration. By 1825 a government committee explained that the members of friendly societies 'do not like to see the management in hands other than their own; and they have an undefined apprehension of an invasion of their funds by the government.'

The friendly societies of all types were a mechanism for collective self-help and mutual support. They did not suffer from the taint of charity and philanthropy, which was something controlled and operated by the wealthy, and all too often experienced as demeaning and degrading by the beneficiaries of charity or benevolence. The friendly societies represented something altogether different: self-reliance. Eventually, friendly societies constituted the largest set of voluntary associations in Britain, reaching by 1904 about six million members, equivalent to one-half of all adult males.

And by then the friendly societies had established the organisational basis for trade unions and co-operative societies, and for a flowering of community business in the industrial age, as we shall see in later chapters.

While the guilds were superseded, they were never entirely forgotten, although later scholars have disagreed about their historical significance. For some, they were seen as a deplorable barrier to economic and social progress, for others, a positive and wholly beneficiary means to achieve this.

Adam Smith and Karl Marx were among those who were, from very different perspectives, to condemn the guild system. Adam Smith regarded the guilds as a barrier to free competition, because they allowed 'the freemen of a corporation to hinder the rest of the inhabitants from employing any workmen but themselves.' Marx on the other hand regarded guilds as an embodiment of class conflict, in which 'guild-master and journeyman, in a word, oppressor and oppressed, stood in constant opposition to one another.'

At various times in its history, community business has continued to meet with resistance from these ideological positions, attracting criticism from devotees of the free market who oppose anything that appears to disrupt competition, while also encountering the hostility of municipal socialists, who regard community business as a challenge to state ownership and control, and suspect that it represents a fundamentally capitalist approach to social change.

Yet in late Victorian times, social reformers seeking alternatives to the social evils produced by mass capitalism looked back to the guilds with an appreciative gaze. As we shall see, John Ruskin's 'Guild of St George' was to prove influential in the development of a generation of craft-based community businesses. And the Anarchist philosopher Kropotkin found in the medieval city, with its guilds and public works, a system of mutual aid which was capable of creating a thriving and prosperous community without the intervention of the State:

> 'In short, the more we begin to know the mediaeval city the more we see that it was not simply a political organisation for the protection of certain political liberties. It was an attempt at organising, on a much grander scale than in a village community, a close union for mutual aid and support, for consumption and production, and for social life altogether, without imposing upon men the fetters of the State, but giving full liberty of expression to the creative genius of each separate group of individuals in art, crafts, science, commerce, and political organisation.'

So the guilds, many centuries after their heyday, came to be seen as a prefiguration of a radically different society founded on principles of universal co-operation, where community and commercial interests would flourish in harmony, to the benefit of all citizens.

PART TWO:
COMMUNITY BUSINESS
IN AN AGE OF POSSIBILITY

As the feudal system disintegrated ideas, people started to imagine how the social order could be redesigned for the benefit of all, and the first attempts at modeling radical community living took place, sowing new seeds for community business.

The settled feudal order could not last. Rural society struggled to recover from the Black Death, which arrived in 1348, and the hardship and grievance brought about by the enclosure of common land. The common people repeatedly challenged the status-quo, and from Wat Tyler onwards a series of popular rebellions took place over the next two centuries. Secular hopes for social revolution fused with millenarian fantasies of a Heaven on Earth, always imminent, always postponed. Suppressed with great ruthlessness, the spirit of rebellion was never wholly quenched.

There was also an emerging humanist philosophy among the small intellectual elite which challenged the legitimacy of the central pillars of the feudal system. Strict censorship was imposed, but the new ideas proved contagious and impossible to contain. One work in particular, Thomas More's Utopia, first published in 1516, was to reverberate down the generations, with its vision of a new kind of community, where people lived, ate, and worked together, where property was shared for the benefit of all, and where education was for everyone, women as well as men. The philosophical underpinning of More and later thinkers who developed his ideas gave social radicals the intellectual tools to challenge the orthodoxy of the period and imagine a different future.

Eventually in the mid-1600s a growing merchant class, seeking a greater role in making the laws which would safeguard their property and their freedom to worship in the way they chose, came into collision with the monarchy, the land-owning nobility and the established church. The institution of elected Parliaments could not be reconciled with the divine right of kings, and the English Civil War broke out.

Eventually the Parliamentarian side triumphed, but in the meantime its New Model Army had become a breeding ground for a multitude of radical groups. Foremost among them were the Levellers, who campaigned for universal suffrage and annual elections, a form of democracy which went far beyond anything which Cromwell and his fellow Parliamentarians had envisaged.

One group of radicals, the Diggers, began to occupy wasteland and to form small experimental communities, with a view to creating a very different kind of society, in which business and trade would be to the benefit of all, and the land would become the 'common Treasury' of the people. As with the Levellers, they were tolerated at first, but when the full implications of their ideas became apparent, were quickly suppressed.

But another group of non-conforming radicals, the Quakers, did survive, and one of them, John Bellers, formed a plan for Colleges of Industry which was to have a seminal influence on the later Co-operative movement. Quakers became renowned as exceptional businessmen, combining entrepreneurial acumen with high moral purpose, and established model communities for their workforces from the late 1600s onwards, playing an important role in the history of community business.

The restoration of the monarchy was followed in 1688 by the Glorious Revolution, a settlement between the Crown and Parliament, which in many respects has endured to this day. It was accompanied by a development of a regulated stock market, and this vastly increased the investment available for business ventures, colonial expansion, and the slave trade. During the 1700's a growing middle class, comfortable in their prosperity and their sense of moral superiority, would cultivate the liberal arts and establish philanthropic institutions for the benefit of the less fortunate.

It was described as an Age of Enlightenment, but not everyone saw it that way, and remnants of the more radical ideas persisted, not least the notion that social improvement could be achieved through a combination of self-organising communities and businesses established for social purpose. Fresh experiments took place, including a 'colony' of Moravians in Yorkshire, where women as well as men played a leading role.

A vision of utopia

In the early 1500s England was one of the most prosperous countries in Europe, but the disintegration of the feudal system had nevertheless produced widespread destitution, especially in the rural population. At the time Thomas More's famous work *Utopia* was first published in 1516, many villages and small towns were derelict, and beggars roamed the country. Thomas More laid much of the blame on the enclosure by private landlords of common land, which rural communities had depended upon since time immemorial for communal grazing and haymaking, as well as foraging for wild produce and for winter fuel.

What was to be done? As a young man Thomas More was a lawyer and part of the intellectual circle which included the humanist philosopher Erasmus. He was able to draw upon the most advanced thinking from across Europe, as well as delve deeply into the texts of ancient Greece and Rome. Thomas More's conclusion, as set out in Utopia, was that improvement in society required a radical and wholesale change to the fundamental principles of property ownership. He argued that the poor were more worthy to enjoy goods and property than the rich because they contributed more through their labour, and asserted that individual property ownership was the primary cause of distress and should be abolished.

The society proposed by Thomas More in his imaginary island of Utopia was ruled by a Prince and magistrates and had many authoritarian features. Order and discipline were more important than liberty. For women especially this was no earthly paradise, and an inflexible hierarchy held sway: 'the oldest man of every family is its governor, wives serve their husbands, and children their parents, and always the younger serves the elder.' Those who broke the law would be turned into slaves, bound in chains, and kept at perpetual labour.

But there was religious toleration and universal education, for women as well as men. Everyone would learn a particular skill: 'Besides agriculture, which is so common to them all, every man has some peculiar trade to which he applies himself, such as the manufacture of wool, or flax, masonry, smith's work, or carpenter's work.' A six-hour working day would be more than sufficient to produce universal prosperity because both men and women would work, idleness would be punished by slavery, and there would be no 'vain and superfluous trades'.

Business was to be carried out by and for the whole community. Produce and manufactured goods would be taken to communal storehouses, where families could simply collect what they needed. More claimed there would be 'no danger of a man's asking for more than he needs.' They would 'have no inducements to do this, since they are sure they shall always be supplied.'

One feature of Utopia, which featured in many later community experiments, was that everyone had the option to eat communally, but was not compelled to do so: 'Though any that will may eat at home, yet none does it willingly, since it is both ridiculous and foolish for any to give themselves the trouble to make ready an ill dinner at home, when there is a much more plentiful one made ready for him so near hand.'

His ideas, and those of numerous followers, were of course not generally adopted. Thomas More himself went on to become Lord Chancellor, and so, ironically, became the upholder of the system of private property and privilege which he had denounced so eloquently as a young man. He became increasingly authoritarian, was responsible for the imprisonment and execution of leading Protestants, and was even accused of personally participating in the torture of suspects. In 1534 he fell into disfavour with Henry VIII, refused to recant, and was executed. The streak of intolerance which was evident in his early writings, and the deeply unpleasant aspects of his later life no doubt reflect the times he lived in. Nevertheless, his refusal to bow to the will of a tyrannical monarch, his denunciation of oppression of the poor by the wealthy, and his Utopian vision of an alternative form of social organisation where people would live on a more equal basis and hold goods in common, made him a beacon for radical dissent for three centuries, and provided an ideological framework which was to inspire and inform community businesses for generations to come.

Little commonwealths

In the mid 17th century, amid the upheavals of the English Civil War and the overthrow of the monarchy, it seemed for a while that everything could change. Demands for a more egalitarian society became more urgent and ever bolder. Out of a multitude of competing ideas and experimentation the seeds were sown for a truly radical form of community business: a common endeavor rooted in local communities where all would share in the generation of wealth, and prosperity would be enjoyed by all.

Pre-eminent among the many 'sectarian' groups which emerged during the Civil War were the Levellers. They believed that all individuals were born into the world with equal rights and they emphasised the sovereignty of the people. They called for extended suffrage, equality before the law, and religious toleration. Moreover, drawing extensively on the ideas set out by Thomas More over a century earlier, they opposed the enclosures of common land: 'all grounds which anciently lay in Common for the poor, and are now impropriate, inclosed and fenced in, may forthwith (in whose hands soever they are) be cast out, and laid open again to the free and common use and benefit of the poor.'

These beliefs found their most radical expression in the activities of a small group of True Levellers, or Diggers as they became known, who occupied a piece of waste land at St George's Hill in Surrey on April Fools' Day in 1649 and started to cultivate it. Their leader Gerrard Winstanley explained their plan: to 'lay the Foundation of making the Earth a Common Treasury for All, both Rich and Poor … Not Inclosing any part into any particular hand, but all as one man, working together, and feeding together.'

St George's Hill was to be only the beginning: Winstanley envisaged a vast series of collective communities taking over all the common land in England. Building further on the ideas of Thomas More, Winstanley believed it would be possible to trade without money, with people co-operating for mutual benefit:

> 'Every tradesman shall fetch materials, as leather, wool, flax, corn and the like, from the public store-houses, to work upon without buying and selling; and when particular works are made, as cloth, shoes, hats and the like, the tradesmen shall bring these particular works to particular shops, as it is now in practice, without buying and selling. And every family as they want such things as they cannot make, they shall go to these shops and fetch without money.'

Commerce, he believed, would thrive under such arrangements: 'Every man shall be brought up in trades and labours, and all trades shall be maintained with more improvement, to the enriching of the commonwealth.'

This was community business in its most radical form, but Winstanley, no doubt drawing on his own experiences at St George's Hill, recognised that it was no easy thing for people to live together harmoniously in a community. He accepted that in any parish 'the body of the people are confused and disordered, because some are wise, some foolish, some subtle and cunning to deceive, others plain-hearted, some strong, some weak, some rash, angry, some mild and quiet-spirited.' Therefore there would be three types of elected official in the community: 'peacemakers' to prevent discord;

'overseers' to maintain order and ensure effective production and exchange; and 'postmasters' to keep monthly records of events and transactions within the parish, and share these records with other parishes and with the nation as a whole.

This system would allow all communities to assist each other in the case of disaster: 'if any part of the land be visited with plague, famine, invasion or insurrection, or any casualties, the other parts of the land may have speedy knowledge, and send relief.' Reports of 'unreasonable action or careless neglect' in one community would help to make other communities more watchful and avoid mistakes. Moreover 'any secret in nature, or new invention in any art or trade or in the tillage of the earth' discovered by one community could be shared with others until eventually 'there will not be any secret in nature which now lies hid.'

This was a compelling vision of what the world might look like: a network of industrious and inventive communities, lending aid to each other at times of distress, and trading and exchanging knowledge for the common good of all.

A movement of Digger communities started to grow. At Wellingborough in Northampton, where over a thousand inhabitants were receiving alms and public relief, nine men led by Richard Smith began 'to bestow their righteous labour upon the common land at Bareshanke.' They resolved not to dig up any man's property 'until they freely give it us' and they were pleased to discover that 'there were not wanting those that did.'

Other Digger colonies were established in Iver in Buckinghamshire, Barnet in Hertfordshire, Enfield in Middlesex, Dunstable in Bedfordshire, among other places. But none of these were given much chance to show what they were capable of. Local landowners and clergymen attacked and destroyed the founding community at St George's Hill, and the other Digger communities were also rapidly suppressed.

The Diggers were not the only people at the time to promote plans of social reform based on community ownership and community trade. In the 1650s Pieter Cornelisz Plockhoy, a Dutch Mennonite, had come to England and proposed to Cromwell a scheme for realising the Christian ideal through a combination of social and industrial effort. In 1659 he published ideas for 'Little Commonwealths' to carry out schemes of co-operative production and housekeeping.

Plockhoy proposed settlements which would house four sorts of people: husbandmen, handicraftsmen, mariners, and masters of arts and sciences. However, his idea of commonwealth was far from inclusive. Only 'rational and impartial persons' would be admitted, he declared. 'All intractable persons, such as those in communion with the Roman see, usurious Jews, English stiff-necked Quakers, Puritans, fool-hardy believers in the Millennium; and obstinate modern pretenders to revelation,' were to be excluded. One hundred families would live together, and Plockhoy believed that this would create economies of scale: 25 women could do the housework, freeing up 75 for other productive labours; less fuel would be needed for cooking, which could be done communally; and 'meat, drink and other things' would cost less because they would be bought in quantity. Everyone would work six hours a day for the benefit of the colony, and the rest of the time could be devoted to private interests.

Cromwell rejected the proposals, and they were never implemented, but Plockhoy's ideas generated great interest among the 'stiff-necked' Quakers, another radical sect which had emerged from the upheavals of the Civil War. And, as we shall now see, the Quakers were to play a significant part in the continuing history of community business.

The early Quakers and plans for a college of industry

After the failure of the English Revolution the story of community business took, at least for a while, a less radical course. But the idea that commercial success could be accompanied by community prosperity was given new and practical impetus by the followers of one of the few factions which survived and regrouped in the post-revolutionary period: the Quakers.

George Fox, the founder of the Quaker movement, wrote in 1669 in his instructions for the society that 'Friends should have and provide a house or houses where an hundred may have rooms to work in, and shops of all sorts of things to sell, and where widows and young women might work and live.'

These ideas clearly draw on those of Plockhoy and probably also of Winstanley, who joined an early Quaker group which included Fox. However, such thinking was quietly dropped as the Quakers abandoned the challenge to private property ownership, seeking instead to find ways to align business endeavours with moral good and public improvement.

In 1695 the Quaker John Bellers published 'Proposals for Raising a College of Industry of all Useful Trades and Husbandry, With Profit to the Rich, A Plentiful Living for the Poor, and a Good Education for Youth, Which will be an Advantage to the Government by the Increase of their People and their Riches.'

Bellers proposed that a community of some three hundred producers should be established and run on a joint stock basis. The College of Industry would be self-supporting and indeed surplus-generating, and in this way would attract commercial investment: 'A thousand Pound is easier raised where there is Profit, than one hundred Pound only upon Charity.' It is an idea echoed by many modern-day proponents of social investment.

No surplus would arise until the requirements of the workers at the college had been amply provided for. Bellers was determined that the College would not bear the stamp of charity: it was to be 'the rich man's debt to the industrious labourer, and not their Charity to them.' Wages would not be paid in money but rather in kind; indeed, Bellers believed that labour rather than money should become the unit of exchange: 'the standard to value all Necessaries by', thus anticipating the time-voucher schemes first introduced a century later.

Bellers advocated the combination of work and education: 'Labour adds Oyl to the Lamp of Life when thinking Inflames it,' he wrote. Education would be accomplished more by object-lesson than by theory, more by practice and experience than by learning by rote.

The College was designed for 300 people. It was intended to serve as an illustration of what was possible, and Bellers believed that the same approach could also work for a community as large as 3,000 people. An attempt was made to put the ideas into practice in Clerkenwell in 1701. Bellers had proposed that men and women of all occupations should work a farm, but the Clerkenwell Workhouse which was set up as a result of his writings was more like a factory. It did not prosper and later became a hospital and nursery, and eventually a school. But nevertheless, the ideas of Bellers were not lost – as we shall see in later chapters his proposals for a College of Industry were to prove seminal in the thinking of Robert Owen a century later and so led eventually to the worldwide co-operative movement.

After the Act of Toleration in 1689, systematic persecution of Quakers reduced, and their belief in self-improvement and hard work, as well as their reputation for honesty, helped them to establish some of the country's most successful businesses across many fields of commerce. Eventually, if you banked with Barclays or Lloyds, took out life insurance with Friends Provident, enjoyed chocolate produced by Cadbury's, Fry's, Terry's, or Rowntree, wore Clarks shoes, ate Huntley and Palmer's biscuits, travelled on the Stockton and Darlington Railway, consulted Bradshaw's railway timetable, drank Barclay Perkins beer, sipped your port from a Waterford Crystal glass, or struck a Bryant and May match, you were, in each and every case, a customer of a Quaker business.

From the early days the Quaker businesses were distinguished by the model communities they built for their workforces, the first of which was in the North Pennines. Here in Alston Moor the London Lead Company, which had been set up by Quakers in 1692, concentrated its operations from the 1750's. A new village, Nenthead, was built for the workforce. The Company went on to provide a school, a reading room, public baths and a wash-house for the miners and their families, and eventually these facilities were opened up not just to employees of the Company, but to the wider community.

The old village inn, the Miners Arms, was purchased by the London Lead Company, and its rent was progressively reduced as trade diminished, with the Company claiming that this was due to 'the miners preferring books to drink.' And indeed Nenthead was the location of one of the first free public libraries in the country, built in 1833. During famine conditions in the 1820s the Company urged the miners to form their own Corn Association, advancing a proportion of wages to allow the miners to purchase corn in bulk. A Ready Money shop was set up, where only cash payments were allowed, in an attempt to drive moneylenders out of the community. Nenthead, like other model communities after it, was providing an opportunity to experiment in creating social change through alternative ways of doing business.

Today the spirit of community business is still alive and well in Nenthead. A group of local people have come together to restore the historic chapel and reopen it as a multipurpose community hub, celebrating the unusual heritage of the village. While the original investments were made by the London Lead company, now new forms of entrepreneurial spirit are helping to fund the project, from the plan to earn income from a cafe and businesses in the space, to a community share issue allowing the villagers of Nenthead to put their own money behind the project.

And as we shall see later on, as the industrial revolution spread so too did the idea that wealthy business owners could establish model communities for their workforces, and that it was in their own interest, as well as that of wider society, that they did so.

For the benefit of the congregation

In 1722 a community was founded at Fulnek (now in the Czech Republic) by the splendidly named Count Nikolaus Ludwig von Zinzendorf. The Fulneck community was formed according to primitive Christian principles, and drew on the doctrines of the original Moravian sect founded by Jan Hus in the fourteenth century. Although personal property was allowed, the community aimed to eliminate divisions between social groups and extremes of wealth and poverty.

In 1743 the Count came to Britain and founded a colony in Yorkshire at Pudsey near Leeds; it was given the name Fulneck. This community included a clothing business, a worsted and glove factory, a farm, a tailor's shop, a shoemaker's, a bakery, a blacksmith, a boarding house, and a general store. The 'Brethren' would weave and dye cloth and the 'Sisters' would work as spinners and later as embroiderers.

Each trade was called a 'diacony' and conducted business for the benefit of the whole congregation. The Methodist preacher John Wesley was impressed with the economic success of Fulneck, and when he visited in 1780 he discovered: 'Above a hundred young men, above fifty young women, many widows, and above a hundred married persons, all of whom are employed from morning to night, without any intermission, in various kinds of manufactures, not for journeymen's wages, but for no wages at all, save a little very plain food and raiment.'

Wesley's account is not entirely accurate, and in fact the manager and the assistants received a small fixed salary. The trading profits went to augment the funds of the congregation and the emphasis was on community benefit not private gain. For example, the community employed a doctor, 'and the object of the gentleman's existence was not to build up a flourishing practice, but to preserve the good health of his beloved Brethren and Sisters'.

Some of the businesses were run in remarkably entrepreneurial ways. John Charlesworth, a Single Brother, was appointed manager of the cloth weaving manufactory, and built up an international trade with Portugal and Russia, creating considerable employment and generating healthy surpluses for the community. But in 1752 he mortgaged the business, speculating £67,000 with a Portuguese financier who suddenly stopped payment, and the money – an enormous sum at the time - was lost. Despite this setback, the sect went on to establish further communities, at Ockbrook in Derbyshire, Gracehill in Ireland, and Dukinfield (later Fairfield) near Manchester.

In 1851 Charles Kingsley pointed to a reason why these communities had prospered while so many others had failed. The Moravians, he claimed, had 'acted up to their own creed, that they were brothers and sisters, members of one body, bound not to care for themselves but for the Commonweal.'

Within these communities a rigid moral law was in operation. Allocation of work tasks, marriages, approval of applications to join the community and other matters were decided by 'lot', an old custom of the Moravians dating back to 1467. Zinzendorf carried a little green book with detachable leaves, each inscribed with a biblical text, and in a dilemma he would pull out a leaf at random for guidance. This system was regarded as the means of revealing the authentic voice of God, and was only abandoned in 1857. Whether better decisions were made before or after this system was given up is not clear.

The inn at Fulneck continued trading until 1819, cloth manufacturing lasted until 1837, and the community bakery until 1846. The community continued to thrive in the 19th and 20th centuries, but refocused its efforts in the field of education rather than manufacture.

Many of the early records of this community still survive. As with community businesses later, there were endless discussions and debates about how the business should be run, and a series of triumphs and setbacks occurred, all of which were meticulously recorded.

An entry for 22 April 1766 records a proposal from Brother Andreas Christian Schloezer, recently arrived from a Moravian congregation in Herrnhut in Saxony, to establish a 'manufactory' of coloured paper. Known as Herrnhut paper, this was celebrated for its rich colours and beauty of design, and was much in demand across Europe.

Three days later the proposal was agreed at a conference of the Brethren who ran the Shop (the community's trading operations) subject to the condition that Schloezer would teach others in the community how to produce the coloured paper. The community was also careful to ensure it would have a monopoly of the new technique: the agreement stated that Schloezer was 'not to show any Person in England besides the Mystery nor to make in three years hence any coloured paper, but in Fulneck'.

At their conference, the Brethen decided that the paper should be produced by the Single Sisters, by which was meant the women who were too young to be married, the spinsters, and the widows.

These would be paid a modest wage, and Schloezer would teach the craft to one of the Sisters, Margaret Woodhouse. The Brethren were confident the women would agree to this, 'which if they do, it is hoped will allow sufficient and more Wages than Spinning'.

However, the single sisters, led by Margaret Woodhouse, were not convinced by these terms, and a subsequent journal entry set out their response: 'it would not be worth their while to work it only for wages'. They wanted a better deal: 'they would have the buying of the Paper, making the Colours, and the manufacturing of it together, else it would not be agreeable to them to take it'.

After several days of tense discussion a settlement was almost reached, that not only wages, but also rent for the workroom and all of the profits at the end of the year, be paid to the Single Sisters, despite the Shop Conference recording that 'we are a little apprehensive of the consequences of an independent spirit gaining too much ground.'

However, David Mathias, who ran the Shop, was firmly against the idea of giving way to the Single Sisters, so the question was put to Lot. As always, three questions were put: whether to agree the proposition, to reject it, or to postpone the decision to a later date. The following Lot was drawn: 'Postpone the settling anything about the Single Sisters making coloured Paper till Brother Petrus comes here'. Three weeks later the matter was discussed again, presumably with Brother Petrus present. Despite long discussion, Mathias refused to budge from his position, so the question was decided by Lot once again. This time the following Lot was drawn: 'The Single Sisters have our Saviour's approbation to take the coloured paper manufactory entirely into their hands,' and so the business began in earnest.

Brother Mathias was quick to save face, and he read out a letter explaining that 'he is willing to be helpful therein, upon the condition that the profit is wholly employed for helping the poor Single Sisters.' The next year, with encouragement from Margaret Woodhouse, he agreed to make trips to Gloucester, Bath, Bristol,

London, Coventry, Birmingham and other places 'with a view to procure custom for the Single Sister's manufacture of marbled paper.'

The workforce grew, offering a means of livelihood to the more infirm members of the community, including Sister Betty Clark 'who having served thirteen years in the kitchen to the wasting of her strength it is hoped this will be an easier occupation of employment to her.'

In October 1767 the accounts of the coloured paper business revealed that a profit of twelve pounds six shillings and sixpence had been achieved. During the 1760's and 1770's marbled paper from Fulneck was sent across the country to be used in bookbinding, for lining boxes and to decorate ink pots.

Margaret Woodhouse died in April 1788, aged 75. The business died with her, and yet it had flourished for 22 years. It was the precursor of the marbled endpapers which became universal in book manufacturing in the succeeding decades, and was an early illustration that community business could operate at the forefront of innovation.

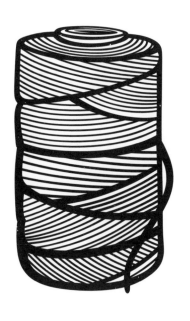

PART THREE:
COMMUNITY BUSINESS
IN THE EARLY INDUSTRIAL AGE

The factory system in various forms had existed since the Elizabethan era, and windmills and watermills had been a source of power since the earliest times. But by the late 1700s a series of new technologies had emerged: John Kay's 'flying shuttle', James Hargreaves' 'spinning jenny', Samuel Crompton's 'mule', Richard Arkwright's 'water frame' and above all James Watts' steam engine, which was capable of generating mechanical power on a scale never before imagined.

Technological innovation was accompanied by rapid market growth, both domestic and international, and mass production of textiles and of an immense range of manufactured goods began in earnest. Towns like Manchester, Birmingham, Sheffield and Bradford expanded rapidly to accommodate the fast-growing industrial workforce.

The Scottish economist Adam Smith showed that, in an industrial factory system, the division of labour in manufactured goods could lead to vast increases in productivity. At the same time he claimed that self-interest pursued under conditions of justice and competition could promote the good of society far more effectively than any form of philanthropy. But life in the slums of the new industrial cities did not seem to bear out this hopeful view. As the 'dark Satanic mills' became an increasingly common feature of the landscape, productivity grew, and immense fortunes were accumulated by successful factory owners, but in many respects the conditions of working people worsened dramatically.

So what was the alternative? It turned out that community business, in various forms, was the answer that many social reformers and working people themselves turned to.

From 1776 Thomas Spence produced a series of pamphlets calling for a new and radical form of localism: a system of self-determining parish communities, where land taxation would be applied for universal health and education, and where a multitude of small businesses would prosper.

A significant advance in the history of community business occurred during the 1790s and early 1800s when milling societies were established on mutual aid principles, with working people buying grain in bulk and even running their own mills. Some operated on a grand scale, harnessing the new steam power, and demonstrating for the first time that the 'lower classes' were capable of running successful business ventures for the benefit of their communities.

One wealthy mill-owner, Robert Owen, not only created a model village for his factory workers, but went much further, seeing to establish nothing less than a 'new moral world'. Rediscovering the ideas of the Quaker John Bellers, he proposed a way to reorder society on the basis of a series of 'villages of co-operation', in which enterprise would be owned in common by the workforce.

The founding principles of the co-operative movement, which persist to this day, aimed to combine the formation of mutual aid businesses with the creation of communities in which co-operative life would be centre stage. While there were many failures, especially at first, eventually a model of co-operative stores emerged which was to prove resilient for the long term. While Owen's ambitions for villages of co-operation were never realised, the co-operative societies were able to build up a widening portfolio of trading activities, in which members of the community as investors, workers and customers were able to share in the surpluses generated.

Furthermore, as working people organised themselves into trade unions and campaigned for a widening of democracy through the Chartist movement, they adapted ideas from the co-operative movement in an attempt to create entrepreneurial communities run by and for working people themselves.

Not mere spectators
in the world

In 1775 a Newcastle schoolmaster, Thomas Spence, gave a lecture to the Newcastle Philosophical Society, arguing that poverty and injustice in an age of rapidly increasing material prosperity were the direct consequence of theft from the people of land, their common inheritance.

Spence's Plan was simple: all land would be reclaimed by the people, and pass into ownership and control of parish corporations, which would be self-governing, and set their own laws, and every adult, male and female, with residence of a year would enjoy full citizenship rights. A radical form of localism indeed. Too radical for the Newcastle Philosophical Society, which promptly expelled him. Too radical for the government of the day, which repeatedly imprisoned him.

In 1792 Spence travelled to London and set up a street stall on Chancery Lane where he sold rum punch and distributed radical propaganda. While in the city, Spence developed his ideas further. Local land taxation would produce sufficient income for all the needs of society, because there would be no need for an expensive and centralised officialdom. Any funds left over would be distributed as equal dividends to all members of the population, the elderly and infants included.

If someone were to arrive in need from a foreign land, they should be provided with relief by the parish, but the cost should be defrayed from the parish contribution to the national exchequer. In this way, refugees would be helped, but not looked upon with 'an envious eye.'

Spence spoke out for the emancipation of women as well as men: he declared that women not only knew their rights 'but have spirit to assert them.' He even proposed that in every parish a committee of women rather than their 'gallant lock-jawed spouses and paramours' would manage the business of collecting rental income and commissioning public works.

Spence believed that commerce would thrive under his system: 'the uncommon freedom, and security of property in such a happy state would operate as a stimulus rather than a check to industry.' Free trade and manufacture, a flourishing agriculture, and localised democracy would combine to raise the nation to a high moral level, a people's Jubilee.

A small circle of followers grew around him, and after he died in 1814, a Society of Spencean Philanthropists was formed, dedicated to bringing Spence's Plan to fruition. Frustrated in their attempts to achieve their aims through rational argument, the Society turned to armed insurrection. This culminated in 1820 in the fiasco of the Cato Street conspiracy, a bungled attempt to assassinate members of the government and the Prime Minister, Lord Liverpool. Many of its leaders were executed or transported.

Spence and his followers had no realistic plan to bring about the wholesale social and political changes they believed were necessary. But nevertheless they had contributed to the ferment of radicalism that flourished in the years following the French

Revolution. In 1791 Tom Paine's *Rights of Man* appeared, followed in 1792 by Mary Wollstonecraft's *A Vindication of the Rights of Woman*. In 1797 Paine published his pamphlet on land reform, *Agrarian Justice*, in which he proposed that all landowners should pay a ground-rent to the community to be accumulated in a national fund. From this fund every person reaching the age of twenty one would receive a bounty of 'Fifteen Pounds Sterling' to enable him, or her, to 'begin in the World.' He also called for a universal old age pension.

However, Paine's proposals did not allow for local community ownership or control. The state, through the national fund, would provide for all. Thomas Spence immediately saw the danger in this. He accused Paine of promoting 'the sneaking unmanly spirit of conscious dependence' and he rejected Paine's confidence in a centralised state, suggesting that local communities are best placed to apply ingenuity to local problems, so that 'we are not mere spectators in the world, but as men ought to be, actors.'

This was the beginning of a debate which was to run and run. Would social reform be best accomplished through a national Parliament and a centralised state, or by means of largely autonomous local communities? Should all people play an active and determining role, as actors rather than spectators, or should authority and resources be controlled by an educated and professionalised elite? This debate remains as relevant and unresolved today as it was in the 1790s, with modern community businesses flying the flag for Spence's belief that action within local communities can often be the best starting point to solve the big problems faced by the country at large.

Milling and mutual aid

In 1795 and 1796 'bread riots' broke out in Tewkesbury, Norwich, Berwick-upon-Tweed, Croydon, Cambridge, Carlisle, Nottingham, Newcastle and many other places across the country. Women played a major role, as an angry population occupied markets and demanded that traders reduce their prices. While there were indeed some attacks on mills and hoarders, and some shipments of grain were seized, the so-called riots were generally peaceful attempts to achieve a fair price, rather than a free market price, for bread. In the notorious slum of Seven Dials in London's Covent Garden a crowd tore down the stall of a baker accused of selling lightweight loaves. When a magistrate intervened he weighed the loaves, agreed with the crowd, and handed out the loaves for free. But in most places the protests ended unhappily when the local militia was called in, and ringleaders were arrested and in some cases executed.

Protest was not the only response. Edmund Burke claimed that the food shortages were accompanied by a great wave of private philanthropy, producing 'a care and superintendence of the poor, far greater than any I remember.' Whether or not that was true, working people were not prepared simply to depend upon the benevolence of the wealthy, and alongside protest and philanthropy, there came a third response: mutual aid.

Friendly societies started by bulk-buying grain for their members in order to keep prices as low as possible. The example had been set as early as 1769 when the Fenwick Weavers friendly society, near Kilmarnock in Ayrshire, started dealing in oatmeal on behalf of its members. This early co-operative model had worked well, and in 1795 'flour clubs' were founded in many parts of the country. For example at Rothley in Leicestershire a friendly society drew £50 from its funds to purchase corn, have it ground, and sell the flour at cost to members.

Sometimes friendly societies banded together to achieve a greater impact. The Sheffield masons, believing that the local friendly societies had 'the power of effecting something very advantageous towards easing the present almost intolerable burthen,' combined with fifteen other societies to purchase grain or flour of the best quality and at the lowest prices. Every member received one stone of flour a week at cost, with an additional half a stone a head for the rest of their family. The saving made by flour club members was typically 4d to 6d per stone, and furthermore the establishment of flour clubs frequently led to a general lowering of flour prices as local millers reacted to the competition.

In order to reduce the price still further some friendly societies took the bold step of establishing their own mills, although they were not the first to do so. Indeed, the first co-operative corn mill probably dates back to 1757, and was built by shipwrights working in the Woolwich docks at another time of wheat scarcity and high prices. Burnt down in 1760, probably as a result of an arson attack by local bakers, the Woolwich mill was rebuilt on a larger scale and appears to have prospered.

Other examples followed. In 1778, when wheat prices were again high at the close of the American wars, several friendly societies in Mansfield contributed to build a post windmill 'for the benefit of families that belong to the members of the different clubs', serving about 1,500 people. So, in the crisis of 1795, the friendly societies had good examples from which they could learn, and they moved quickly. In Sheffield, for example, they took out a twenty one-year lease on a suitable site, and the Club Flour Mill was built, containing two water wheels and eight pairs of stones.

These first co-operative mill societies had all employed wind or water power, a system well suited to small-scale ventures though not for more ambitious projects. But the new steam technology offered a huge opportunity to increase scale and production. The Boulton and Watt experimental corn mill at Soho had already demonstrated viability, and successful steam mills had been set up in Birmingham, Bristol and London. In 1795 the co-operative mill societies were determined to take full advantage of this new technology, but there seemed to be an insuperable obstacle: the capital outlay required was at least £2,000, a considerable amount at the time.

In order to address this daunting challenge, a new form of co-operative venture emerged: the 'union mill society'. Here, the capital for the mill was raised by the sale of shares to the public, augmented in some cases by donations from local benefactors. These organisations were, in effect, unincorporated joint-stock companies, and their legal status was uncertain. But the model certainly worked.

The first was the Anti Mill Society, founded in 1795 by the 'poor inhabitants' of Hull, who sought both approval and financial assistance from the mayor and aldermen of the town. The Anti Mill Society was launched with the aim of raising £2,500 share capital. The initial share price was six shillings and four pence, later rising to £1, there was a limit of five shares per person, and a 5% cash dividend was promised. Provision was made for the purchase of shares in instalments, the Society rules emphasising that the object was 'to make it convenient for the lowest capacity'. Subscribers to the Hull Anti Mill were to pay one shilling and one penny for four weeks and then six pence per week for four weeks.

When £798 had been raised the Society found a builder who was prepared to erect a mill, allowing the Society four years in which to pay the outstanding amount. Payments of six pence per week had to be made by shareholders until the full mill construction costs, plus interest, had been paid off. A large seven-storey mill with adjoining granaries and a mill house was built in 1796, by which time it had 1,435 members, and production commenced the following year.

Support for co-operative milling grew in Hull, and a second union mill society was founded there in 1799. In Birmingham in 1796 more than £6,000 had been promised in shares and donation for a new 16-horsepower steam mill operated by the Birmingham Flour and Bread Company. This had 1,360 shareholders by the year 1800, and at the time it was probably the largest mill in the country. The example was taken up elsewhere, in Manchester, Whitby, Bridlington, Newport, Beverley, and Shardlow. The Good Intent Society near Brentford in Middlesex, for example, raised more than £2,000 and began trading in 1803.

The co-operative mills, whether established by the pooled funds of friendly societies, or by the pioneering community share issues of the union mill societies, generally prospered. Some not only milled the grain to produce flour, but also baked the flour into bread. 38 sacks of flour were baked each week at Birmingham, and holders of five or more shares could have their flour and bread delivered to their houses. A society at Wolverhampton distributed 770 loaves each week, supplying about fifty shops in the area, where members could buy their flour or bread. Cash sales were insisted upon by all societies, to reduce the problem of debt among the industrial poor.

In all, at least 46 flour and bread societies were set up, the majority in the years of great scarcity 1795-96 and 1799-1801, and then later in the economic slump that followed the Napoleonic wars, and some proved to be of considerable duration: the Devonport Union Mill in Plymouth began operations in 1817 and continued to 1892.

The industrialist Matthew Boulton was an active supporter of his local union mill society in Birmingham. He denied suggestions that it was a philanthropic venture, and pointed out its true significance: 'This mill was not erected by the opulent for the benefit of the poor labouring workman, but it was erected principally by the latter class for the benefit of themselves.'

The mill societies mark a turning point in the history of community business. Above all, it was now possible to demonstrate, with examples to be found across the country, that successful community businesses could be run by the 'lower classes', for the benefit of ordinary people. Moreover, they could operate at scale, place themselves at the forefront of innovation, and compete successfully in the most challenging conditions. They offered proof that an alternative to the operations of early industrialism capitalism could exist, an alternative which relied on community solidarity as well as entrepreneurial skill.

A new
moral world

In the early 1800s wealthy mill-owner Robert Owen resolved to do something about the conditions of his workforce and their families at New Lanark in Scotland. He provided better housing and community facilities, and opened a school which he described as an 'Institution for the Formation of Character'. The scheme attracted great interest, and at first Owen expected that his example would be enthusiastically taken up by other wealthy industrialists. It wasn't.

After Owen discovered the ideas of John Bellers, his thinking expanded in new directions. An opportunity came in 1817. Alarmed by mass unemployment in the aftermath of the Napoleonic wars, and a rise in social unrest, the government was desperate for solutions. Owen was invited by the Archbishop of Canterbury and then by a Parliamentary Committee on the Administration of the Poor Laws to set out his ideas.

Owen drew up detailed plans for a 'new moral world': a society made up of a commonwealth of self-governing and self-sufficient 'villages of co-operation', each of around 1,000 people, where sectarian religious views would not be allowed to take hold, and industry and enterprise for the common good would provide prosperity for all. The villages would be located in the centre of farmland, and the layout would maximise a communal way of life. There should be enough land to supply the needs of the village, with a surplus to allow trade with other communities. The Committee published a diagram of Owen's proposals inscribed 'A view and plan of the Agricultural Villages of Unity and Mutual Co-operation'.

A Parliamentary vote was held on whether to establish a select committee to get the plan underway, but the proposal was defeated by 141 votes to 17. Despite this setback Owen's belief in the force of rational persuasion made him confident that capital to create the first communities would come from industrialists, landowners, parishes and counties, and groups of farmers, mechanics and tradesmen. But no one it seemed was prepared to buy in to his vision.

Owen's plans were viewed with alarm by conservatives, who regarded the scheme as irreligious, with some justification, for Owen announced that the communities should not be undermined by the 'gross errors' inherent in the 'fundamental notions of every religion that has hitherto been taught to men'. At the same time the plans were received with suspicion by radicals, who detected a paternalistic tone. William Cobbett feared that the villages of co-operation would produce 'parallelograms of paupers', and an article in the Political Register warned that Owen's plan would 'cover the face of the country with workhouses, to rear up a community of slaves, and consequently to render the labouring part of the People absolutely dependent upon the men of property'. In 1817 Thomas Wooler, editor of the *Black Dwarf*, claimed there was nothing new in the plan, and Hone in the *Reformist's Register* pointed out the debt to Thomas Spence, calling it 'The Spencean Plan doubly dipped'.

In disgust, Owen headed off to the United States. With $135,000 of his own money he purchased an existing colony in Indiana capable of housing 800 people, with the intention to run it on 'co-operative' principles, and called it New Harmony. Owen was determined that the new co-operative settlement should exert an educative force not just on its own inhabitants but on society at large. The key was to attract scientists of the highest calibre and in this Owen was remarkably successful. In 1826 William Maclure, a wealthy Scottish geologist and educationalist, sent out his private library, philosophical instruments, and collections of natural history. These were accompanied by a party of scientific associates, including the geologist Gerhard Troost and the naturalists Charles Lesueur and Thomas Say. They travelled together to New Harmony by keel-boat from Pittsburgh - a 'boat-load of knowledge'.

Maclure's aim was to make New Harmony the 'centre of education in the west'. His enthusiasm had a deep impact on Owen's sons; one of them, David Dale Owen, became a prominent geologist, while another, Robert Dale Owen won election as a Congressman and introduced the Bill which established the Smithsonian Institute. The young Abraham Lincoln saw the colonists pass up the river on their way to New Harmony and unsuccessfully begged his father to let him join them.

One of those who did join the community was Josiah Warren, an American anarchist who went on to establish the first time store in Cincinnati in 1827, where hours rather than dollars were the medium of exchange, and goods were purchased with labour notes. Warren coined the phrase 'cost the limit of price', meaning that the price of goods should never be higher than the value of the labour which went into them. This would be measured by hours worked, with adjustments for difficulty and disagreeableness of the work performed. The prices in his time store increased the longer the time that a customer spent with the shopkeeper as shown by a timer dial, and this measure helped the store to become profitable. Something similar had been attempted in New Harmony, where members of the colony had been expected to render services to the community in exchange for credit at the town's store.

It was the beginning of time-banking – an idea that has seen a widespread revival in modern times.

In 1821 George Mudie, a follower of Robert Owen, established a Co-operative and Economical Society, and settled 21 families in rented property in Spa Fields in Islington. The community pooled resources for communal meals, domestic services, and childcare, maintained a printing press, and ran a pioneering community health centre. To encourage 'self-criticism' monitors were chosen by the members to 'admonish' those who offended against the 'general harmony and goodwill of the families'. A notice advertised the following businesses: carving, gilding, boots and shoes, gentlemen's clothes, dressmaking, millinery, umbrellas, hardware (including stoves, kettles, etc.), cutlery and 'transparent landscape window blinds', and earnings from the businesses were pooled for the benefit of all.

The movement was seething with ideas, not all of them practical. In 1834 a letter was published in Owen's magazine the *New Moral World* proposing a 'Floating Co-operative Community' which was to be moored on the Thames, where it was thought the inhabitants would be safe from the extortions of retail traders, lodging-house keepers, and gin shops. Also in 1834 the first women's co-operative association was formed with the objective of forming 'associative homes' with families living in terraced dwellings. To raise funds they started to trade in tea and coffee, inviting the supporters of the co-operative movement to buy their goods.

In the same year it was reported that community coffee-houses existed in London; it was the beginning of a long tradition of community cafes and restaurants stretching to the present day. At the time community coffee houses and cafes often operated in shabby surroundings, were usually designed first and foremost to provide low cost meals to the very poorest, and failed to attract a wider customer base. This proved to be a precarious model and few survived for very long.

In 1826 at Orbiston in Scotland another more substantial community was established near Hamilton on 291 acres by the banks of the river Calder. Its founder was Abram Combe, a successful Edinburgh tanner, who had visited New Lanark and decided to devote his life and his fortune to the pursuit of Robert Owen's ideas.

The plans were ambitious. The centrepiece was a five storey block to house 200 families with their 400 children, containing a kitchen, bakehouse, library, drawing rooms, workshops, theatre, and school. On the first anniversary of the community, self-government was introduced; all matters would be decided upon at a weekly general meeting. An ethical code of conduct was drawn up which incorporated the Sermon on the Mount and additional clauses relating to temperance, cleanliness and the sanctity of private rooms. However, Combe was described as a man 'without any sense of art in his soul,' the large buildings were severe and plain, completely lacking in ornamentation, and for convenience, every member was given a number by which he or she was to be known.

In October 1826 a handbill was produced, advertising the services which the Orbiston community was able to offer, and on paper at least it was an impressive catalogue of skills and trades, from familiar occupations such as printing, bookbinding, shoemaking, carving, painting, tailoring, upholstery and weaving, to more specialist activities like carriage wheel making, snuff box repair and 'superior blacking' of boots.

The Orbiston handbill also made the claim that the co-operative model of production, by providing an association of many skills, would result in products of a superior quality:

> 'The public will perceive that the trades enumerated above will, at times, command the great advantages that a union of labour and interest can give to forward any operation required. In general society it too often occurs that an opposition of interests prevents some part of an undertaking from having the same superior skill employed in the execution of it that the rest may have; but in this establishment the united intelligence of the whole body will be always employed, either in forwarding

their respective occupations, or concentrated when necessary, to any given operation. This superiority can only be found amongst persons united for the mutual benefit of each other.'

Despite the initial optimism, the community at Orbiston remained vulnerable to the vagaries of fortune. Abram Combe died in 1827, and the community came to an untimely end when his brother, who took over the property, ordered the members to quit.

Altogether there were 16 communities in America (in Indiana, Ohio, New York County, Pennsylvania, Tennessee, and Wisconsin) and ten in Britain associated directly or indirectly with Owen. The most promising was in Ireland at Ralahine in County Clare. In 1831 an Irish landowner John Vandeleur invited Thomas Craig who had worked with Abram Combe at the Orbiston community to establish a co-operative society on his estate of 618 acres. The Ralahine community consisted of 46 people and would be self-governing: a managing committee of nine would be elected twice a year.

The community drew on the experiments of Josiah Warren, and created another early version of a time bank. Instead of money the workers were paid in cardboard vouchers representing a day's work which could be spent in a co-operative store, so ensuring that wealth as far as possible remained in circulation within the community. If the members wished to spend money outside the community they could exchange the labour notes for coin. All members over the age of 17 took a share in the division of profits.

The estate prospered and a further twenty-nine people joined. The first mowing machine in Ireland was introduced. Unfortunately, the landowner lost all his possessions through gambling, and because he had retained ownership of the estate, the land was seized and the community was evicted. It was an early lesson in the importance of community ownership and control of land and buildings in a community business, and one which remains of continuing importance in modern times.

Another attempt was made by Robert Owen himself. In 1839 he rented the Queenwood Farm at East Tytherly in Hampshire, where he built a large three-storey building with 80 rooms and named it Harmony Hall. No expense was spared, and its kitchens were of London hotel standard. In one of his more grandiose gestures, Owen had the initials 'CM' inserted in flint in the brickwork of the building, standing for 'Commencement of the Millennium.' The estate was designed to accommodate 700 people but at its height there were never more than 100 residents and the venture was declared bankrupt in 1845.

As can be seen, few of these early communities lasted long. Robert Owen's son Robert Dale Owen was later to explain why New Harmony failed after just three years. Its members, he said, were 'a heterogeneous collection of radicals, enthusiastic devotees to principle, honest latitudinarians, and lazy theorists, with a sprinkling of unprincipled sharpers thrown in.' In hindsight, he believed, failure was inevitable: 'all cooperative schemes which provide equal remuneration to the skilled and industrious and the ignorant and idle must work their own downfall, for by this unjust plan, they must of necessity eliminate the valuable members and retain only the improvident, unskilled, and vicious.'

As George Jacob Holyoake, the first historian of the co-operative movement was to write, all too often a co-operative community 'was regarded in social mechanics then as a sort of flying machine, and it fulfilled the expectation of the day by falling down like one.' Since those times, flying machines have turned out to be an entirely practical proposition, as indeed have many forms of co-operative community business, but the idealised co-operative communities proposed by Owen and his early followers were never to establish themselves on any scale and Owen's vision that the whole of society could be re-organised as network of co-operative villages was not to be realised.

Robert Owen was certainly not without weakness. He mistrusted the abilities of the working classes to manage any large scale enterprise themselves, and believed in the necessity of middle-class leadership in community experiments. His tendency towards conservatism and elitism often threatened to hold back the popular development of the movement.

But Owenism forged ahead in spite of Owen. He had laid the foundation of a form of 'socialism' based on harmonious self-sustaining communities, organised on social principles, and capable of running community businesses. This was the original meaning of the term socialism in England, although later the word was to be mainly associated with Marxism and Fabianism, in both cases ideologies that assumed that progress would be only achieved by an enlightened bureaucracy delivering universal services though a centralised state.

Although Owenite socialism was dismissed as naive by some, and threatening by others, and although it was easy to dismiss the first experiments of Owen and his followers as failures, the co-operative ideal proved to be remarkably durable. Co-operative societies were established in every part of the country, and gave rise to a worldwide movement, which endured through all the vicissitudes of the 19th and 20th centuries, and which continues to this day.

In New Harmony, Owen had proposed a new role for women. With child-rearing, cooking and washing transferred to the community, women could play a role in factories and gardens, and take an equal share in communal tasks. Owen also took a reforming position on marriage, attacking impediments to divorce, and for this he was much condemned by the establishment. Owen was not the first to combine the political and social emancipation of women with proposals for a society based on small communities. Mary Wollstonecraft in 1790 and Thomas Spence in 1797 had sketched out just such a vision. But it was Owen and his followers who were to develop these ideas further and indeed attempt to put them into practice. The atheist Emma Martin believed that only Owenite socialism could remove the great evil of the 'depraved and ignorant condition of women' and William Thompson saw in co-operative communities the means to achieve perfect equality between men and women: 'This scheme of social happiness is the only one which will completely and forever ensure the perfect equality and entire reciprocity of happiness between women and men.'

In practice, Owenite communities fell far short of perfection; while women usually had voting rights within the communities, and benefited from education on an equal basis, the apportionment of labour often resulted in women working longer hours, and the leadership of Owenite communities remained heavily male-dominated. It was a pattern which was to persist throughout the development of the co-operative movement and indeed other forms of community business. It is only in very recent times that the balance has shifted to any significant extent; in 2015 a State of Social Enterprise survey revealed that 40% of leaders of social enterprises are now women, a figure which compares well to the private sector, where women comprise only 18% of the leaders of small businesses.

A common interest and a common tie

The Owenite experiments gave birth to a movement of co-operative stores. In 1827 Dr William King became convinced that a co-operative shop could provide the money to finance a community, and set one up in Brighton for this purpose.

Just three years later it was reported that already 300 were operating across the country. A co-operative journal *Common Sense* described their purpose: 'The object of a Trading Association is briefly this: to furnish most of the articles of food in ordinary consumption to its members, and to accumulate a fund for the purpose of renting land for cultivation, and the formation thereon of a co-operative community.'

These objectives were ambitious, but the stores were under-capitalised, and in some cases the early co-operators lacked the knowledge and skills to manage a successful business and to build up a sufficient customer base. Within a decade most had failed.

On May Day 1832 Robert Owen and a group of followers opened 'with some pomp' the first National Equitable Labour Exchange in Charlotte Street, off Grays Inn Road, London. The building was magnificent: it could accommodate nearly 12,000 people. This was to be the first of a series of 'bazaars' to enable working people to exchange articles they had made among themselves.

Labour notes were used for currency. 'The shoemaker brought his pair of shoes to the bazaar, with an invoice of the cost (calculated at six pence per hour). The labour note, of so many hours' value, was given to the shoemaker, who could then, or at any other time, buy with them any other deposit in the bazaar—a hat, or teakettle, or a joint of meat, if he found what he wanted.'

The first day the deposits were 18,000 hours and the exchanges 900 hours. At its height, it was claimed that deposits equivalent to a monetary value of £10,000 a week were made. A Surrey branch was set up in Blackfriars Road, and a Birmingham branch in Coach Yard, Bull Street. The halls were in continual use and on Sundays lectures were given to propagate knowledge among the working classes.

A further opportunity for the social exchange of goods was presented by the Co-operative Congress in Liverpool in October 1832. Delegates brought goods from across the country: 'from Sheffield, cutlery and coffee pots; from Leicester, stockings and lace; from Huddersfield, waistcoat pieces and shawls; from Rochdale, flannels. There were diapers from Barnsley, stuffs from Halifax, shoes and clogs from Kendal, and prints from Birkacre.'

However, the 'bazaars' soon found themselves operating in a difficult and indeed hostile commercial environment. Without textiles from factories and food from farms the Equitable Labour Exchanges could not become self-sufficient. Efforts were made to obtain supplies of bread, meat, provisions and coals, but food and raw materials remained largely outside the system. Also, the labour note system was not insulated from the pressures of the commercial world outside: cash was exchanged for labour notes, and the labour hour was linked to the standard commercial rate of six pence, with adjustments made for workers whose standard rate was higher.

Moreover, the Exchanges became a dumping ground for unsaleable items. Local shopkeepers sent down worthless stock, exchanged it for labour notes, and carried away the pick of the saleable goods, with which they stocked their shops. There were other problems too. The premises were leased, not owned, and when the owner of the Exchange at Grays Inn Road wanted it back he hired 64 men to smash the place up. Within 18 months the experiment was at an end. Even so, the experiment was not entirely unsuccessful. When the Birmingham branch was wound up a surplus of about £8 was paid to the Birmingham General Hospital.

In 1844 new life was imparted into this movement by a group of 28 weavers and other working people who set up The Rochdale Society of Equitable Pioneers opening a small grocery store in Toad Lane, selling only unadulterated goods. They invented a new form of business, whereby the customer became a partner in the rewards of mutual endeavour: they refused to give credit to customers, but for the first time paid them a share of profits (a 'dividend'). The Rules of the Society became a model for others, and within a decade there were nearly 1,000 co-operative stores operating on similar principles across the country.

The Rochdale Society encountered many problems in its formative years, but the characters of the initial pioneers were decisive in overcoming these problems, and not least of their qualities was humour. As George Jacob Holyoake recalled, 'James Smithies was its earliest secretary and counsellor. In the presence of his vivacity no one could despond, confronted by his buoyant humour no one could be angry. He laughed the store out of despair into prosperity.'

In his 1875 work *Thrift*, the popular economist Samuel Smiles praised the success of the Rochdale Pioneers.

> 'The society grew. It established a store for the sale of food, firing, clothes, and other necessaries. In a few years the members set

on foot the Co-operative Corn-mill. They increased the capital by the issue of one-pound shares, and began to make and sell clothes and shoes. They also sold drapery. But the principal trade consisted in the purchase and sale of provisions—butchers' meat, groceries, flour, and such-like. Notwithstanding the great distress during the period of the cotton famine, the society continued to prosper. From the first, it set apart a portion of its funds for educational purposes, and established a news-room, and a library, which now contains over six thousand volumes. The society continued to increase until it possessed eleven branches for the sale of goods and stores in or near Rochdale, besides the original office in Toad Lane. At the end of 1866, it had 6,246 members, and a capital of £99,908. Its income for goods sold and cash received during the year was £249,122; and the gross profit £31,931.'

William King described the virtues of the co-operative model, which allowed working people to pool their efforts and thereby achieve more. But, he stressed, this required a community of people who shared common purpose: 'before many can work, they must join hand in hand: they must know their object and feel a common interest and a common tie.' If any of these elements were missing, the co-operative endeavour would fail. A useful reminder for co-operatives then, and for community businesses today.

Many of the co-operative societies emerged out of the earlier friendly society model, and indeed the legislation which permitted the establishment of friendly societies was used extensively by co-operative ventures.

The co-operative movement also drew on the earlier traditions of flour clubs and milling societies. In 1816 dockworkers on the Medway formed the Sheerness Economical Society 'for obtaining for themselves and families a supply of wheaten bread and flour and butcher's meat'. This eventually led to the Sheerness Co-operative Society, which opened its first shop in the High Street in

1850, an occasion marked by a procession though the town led by a wooden-legged standard bearer carrying the banner of the True Britons Benefit Society. During the next fifty years the Sheerness Co-operative Society opened shops in the local neighbourhoods of Mile Town, Blue Town, Marine Town, Minster, Queenborough and Halfway providing grocery, butchery, drapery, furnishings, boots and shoes, coal, shipping, building, and savings facilities.

The range of business activities operated by the Victorian co-operative societies was remarkable. In Ipswich for example the Industrial Co-operative Society was established in 1867, and with 114 members and £80 capital opened a small grocery store. For the first three years its existence was precarious and dividends to members were low or even at times non-existent. But by 1874 sales from the store had grown to over £5,000, membership stood at 371, and share capital had increased to £579. The Society was then able to purchase a larger site, build a warehouse and bakery, and establish an outfitting department.

In the 1880s it went on to set up a butchery business and also retail outlets in the rural districts of East Suffolk. A large Co-operative Hall was opened in the centre of Ipswich in 1886, and between 700 and 800 members of the Society celebrated with a 'good substantial meal' followed by songs and recitations.

The following year the Ipswich Society took out a lease on a 300 acre farm and in 1892 built four houses on the farm land to accommodate the farmworkers and their families. In 1897 the Society changed its rules to allow the provision of home loans to members 'to enable them to become house owners and thus obtain security of tenure and freedom from disturbance from arbitrary landlords'. At times of hardship the Society was able to set aside funds for the relief of distressed families and in 1897 all employees were granted six days holiday per annum.

In the early 1900s a fleet of vans was purchased to increase rural deliveries, new retail buildings were purchased across the district, and the bakery was upgraded with the latest gas-fired ovens.

So, from small beginnings in a single shop, the co-operative in Ipswich, as in many other places, was able to expand its operations over the years, building its asset base and its sphere of operations, and providing a far-reaching and extensive combination of services, employment and welfare assistance to the community, all controlled and run by local people for themselves. It was a multi-dimensional business model which continues to have resonance today, most notably in the work of development trusts and other types of 'community hub' organisations which aim over time to lift up whole communities by their own efforts.

Fustian jackets, blistered hands and unshorn chins

William Thompson, an Irish economist, political writer, and supporter of female emancipation, was one of the first utopian socialists to believe in the ability of the working class to create its own future. Thompson believed that working people would need to finance their own schemes rather than rely on sympathetic capitalists and that the workers in any co-operative community should have the security of ownership of the community's land and capital property. In 1830 Thompson published *'Practical Directions for the Speedy and Economical Establishment of Communities, on the principles of Mutual Cooperation, United Possessions and Equality of Exertions and of the Means of Enjoyment,'* **in which he remarked: 'If done without any aid from the rich and idle, how animating to the industrious classes! – to the rich, the selfish, what a humiliating reproach!'**

He hoped his instructions would make the establishment of co-operative communities as easy as that of 'any ordinary manufacture'. He also believed that communities would provide markets for each other, and that commerce would flourish as a result, with consequences entirely beneficial to society. He foresaw the perils of globalisation: 'the vain search after foreign markets throughout the globe, no sooner found than over-stocked and glutted by the restless competition of the starving producers'. In contrast to this he believed that working people, through a 'voluntary union of the industrious or productive classes' would be able to establish a more sustainable economy 'by working together for each other, for the mutual supply, directly by themselves, of all their most indispensable wants, in the way of food, clothing, dwelling, and furniture.'

One of the most remarkable illustrations that 'ordinary' working people could establish and manage their community, and operate a successful micro-economy on their own terms, was to be found in the early 1800s in a small neighbourhood of Hastings which became known as the America Ground.

Here, on a strip of shingle shoreline, an unregulated community of up to a thousand people lived. It included a carpenter, miller, maker, and brewer. There were lime kilns and stone masons, lodging houses and pig keepers. A long rope walk was established, so that strands of material could be twisted to manufacture lengths of rope. There was a 'gin palace' and even a school.

The strip of land had been formed by storm surges and there were no legal owners, and as a result the inhabitants paid no rates or taxes. The municipal authorities attempted to take control, but in an extraordinary act of defiance the community raised the Stars and Stripes, proclaiming themselves the 24th State of the United States of America. It was, in effect, their declaration of independence and this why the area became known as the America Ground.

In 1827, five commissioners and twelve jurymen met at the George Hotel at Battle and decide that the lands should be seized on behalf of the King. By 1835 the whole community was cleared.

But today, a community business thrives at Rock House, situated within the old America Ground. The nine floors of Rock House are home to living space, work space, and a community hub. One criteria for those who live and work at Rock House is that they bring enthusiasm, and another is that they make a contribution to the life of the building and to the wider community. And just along the coast is the Hastings pier, rescued after a disastrous fire and brought into community ownership in 2013. Both of these modern-day community businesses see themselves as following in the footsteps of the first inhabitants of the America Ground: resourceful, entrepreneurial, fighting for their community, and proud of it.

Several early trade unions attempted to establish communities where working people could live in prosperity and dignity, emancipated from the industrial slums, drawing on their own financial resources rather than going cap in hand to the state or to wealthy philanthropists.

In 1844 William Evans, who ran a newsagent's shop in Shelton where he sold works by Wollstonecraft, Rousseau and Emerson, proposed to the newly formed Trades Union of Operative Potters that they throw their financial resources into a Joint Stock Emigration Company, to establish a model community in Illinois. He aimed to persuade 5,000 potters to buy a £1 share in the scheme, paying a shilling a week, producing a working capital of £5,000. By October 1844 all the potters' lodges had voted in favour of the scheme, and subscriptions were collected. Emigrants were to be chosen by ballot when subscriptions reached each successive £50 level. They would arrive to find a cabin built for them, five acres of land sowed with wheat and corn, and fifteen acres awaiting cultivation.

This proved no hollow promise. The Union bought 1,600 acres of land in Wisconsin and settled 134 of its members. Unfortunately, back in the Potteries, the unity of the pottery workers fell apart when a rival union was established. There was also discord in Wisconsin about allocation of the land, which impeded the process of legalising the potters' claim. The immigrants complained of the heat, the water, the Indians, and the sandy soil. In June 1850 a meeting of settlers in Fort Winnebago alleged misrepresentation, corruption and incompetence. By January 1851 the Emigration Society was abandoned, and the trade union movement in the Potteries was set back many years.

Elsewhere other trades unions took up the idea of land colonies. In Sheffield around 1848 the Edge Tool Grinders acquired a farm of sixty-eight acres at Wincobank 'with a view to employing their surplus hands,' and the File Hardeners acquired a similar farm elsewhere. The Britannia Metal Smiths established an eleven-acre farm at Gleadless Common Side, employing a manager and a dozen men who supplied a shop which sold the produce at market prices. Employees were paid fourteen shillings a week with six pence for each dependent child. But it seemed that impoverished factory workers rarely made good farm workers, and the colonies failed to prosper.

Although the trade unionists abandoned the attempt to establish co-operative communities, the idea was revived in spectacular fashion by the Chartist leader Feargus O'Connor. Between 1846 and 1848 he founded no less than five villages, starting with O'Connorville (now Heronsgate) on the outskirts of London, and resettling 250 working people from the slums of Victorian England.

The first great Chartist petition had called for universal suffrage, was nearly three miles long and contained 1,280,000 signatures, but had been rejected by Parliament. O'Connor's Land Plan aimed to achieve the right to vote by a different route: when enough working people had obtained property qualifications, the people would be able to vote themselves the reforms which those in power had denied them.

O'Connor broadcast his ideas through his weekly paper the

Northern Star, addressing himself to working people directly: 'the Fustian Jackets, Blistered Hands and Unshorn Chins' as he called them. As O'Connor and his followers threw themselves into the Land Plan, the project took on a life of its own. Most impressively, all the investment to create these villages was drawn from working people themselves, in effect a community share issue on a nationwide scale. O'Connor set up a Land and Labour Bank, and 70,000 working people from the slums of the industrial cities raised nearly £100,000. Those who bought shares, and the lucky few who were awarded homes in ballots for the first model villages, were drawn from every conceivable trade:

> 'Coalminer, weaver, labourer, calico printer, shoemaker, limeburner, block printer, stockinger, baker, woolcomber, innkeeper, smith, tailor, stonecutter, cabinetmaker, joiner, potter, cordwainer, mason, grocer, piecer, moulder, nailer, victualler, postman, skinner, butcher, embroiderer, farmer, hatter, spinner, milkman, servant, gardener, lacemaker, overlooker, warehousemen, tinman, clerk, thatcher, plumber, painter, plasterer, mechanic, clothier, fustian cutter, grinder, bricklayer, trunkmaker, seamstress, warper, turner, carpenter, slater, schoolmistress, cotton band maker.'

O'Connor insisted that he intended no socialism (on the Owenite model) nor partnership with the state. Ownership and control were eventually to reside with the individual, and O'Connor described himself as an 'elevator' not a 'leveller'.

The Chartist villages provided not only decent housing, but also the means to sustain a decent livelihood: a smallholding sufficient to grow enough food to feed a family and to produce a surplus which could be sold in local markets. The model cottages at O'Connorville had three rooms to live in as well as outhouses for a livestock and farming equipment, which were provided by the company together with fruit trees and a supply of manure. O'Connor was determined that quality should be high and the cottages were roomy, well lit, with oak plank floors and good cast iron grates. As the village was being built, working people holding shares would turn up from all over England, finger the seasoned oak, and exclaim 'Eh! But that's rare stuff!'

The transition to rural life was difficult for many of the new settlers, but initial enthusiasm was high and by 1848 some of the allotments were, literally, bearing fruit. One claimed to have 700 fruit-bearing trees: apples, pears, gooseberries and currants. A variety of trading activities soon emerged. At Great Dodford the settlers cultivated strawberries and made jam for sale in markets in Bromsgrove and Birmingham. At Lowbands and Snigs End market gardens were developed to supply Gloucester. At O'Connorville some residents became cobblers and carpenters, providing services to the agricultural community. Outbuildings were sometimes converted into small workshops, and at Great Dodford wives and daughters started making bonnets. Some allottees demonstrated a sound business sense, co-operating to buy coal and groceries at wholesale prices.

But O'Connor himself started feeling the strain. He had stood for Parliament to publicise his cause, and had won a famous victory in Nottingham, but like many a community business leader of today he found himself doing too much of everything, describing himself as 'bailiff, contractor, architect, engineer, surveyor, farmer, dungmaker, cow and pig jobber, milkman, horse jobber and Member of Parliament.'

In the end, this visionary scheme was defeated by attacks by a hostile press, attempts to discredit the concept by commissioners of the hated Poor Law, and refusal of Parliament to allow the company legal status. It was declared an illegal lottery, and in 1851 the Land Company was wound down. By then O'Connor was said to be drinking heavily, and this defeat was too much too bear. After assaulting a policeman in the Strand in 1852 he was arrested and later taken to a clinic for the insane at Chiswick. He considered himself a state prisoner, and regarded his confinement with 'grave pride.' He died in 1855, and the dream of the Chartist Land Plan died with him.

PART FOUR:
COMMUNITY BUSINESS
IN A LATER INDUSTRIAL AGE

As industrialisation continued, some limited measures were taken to ameliorate the conditions of the industrial poor. The Factory Act in 1833 and the Mines Act in 1842 prohibited the employment of children younger than nine years of age and limited the hours that children between nine and 13 could work, while the Elementary Education Act in 1870 provided for free education of all children between five and 12 in England and Wales. Another major step was achieved in 1871 when trade unions were decriminalised.

As the movement of friendly societies and co-operatives grew in strength a new form of community business emerged by means of which working people were able to pool finance and acquire decent homes: the building society. These were successful, so much so that legislation was passed in 1836 to permit private investment, and while this enabled rapid expansion, it also eroded their connection with local communities.

The appalling housing conditions in industrial towns and cities attracted the interest of philanthropists, and Lord Shaftesbury, George Peabody, Sir Edward Cecil Guinesss and others established foundations to provide decent homes for the industrious poor. Their 'five percent philanthropy' model was designed to offer a sound return to commercial investors at the same time as doing good. They laid the foundation for the housing association movement.

During the 19th century and beyond a series of wealthy industrialists and philanthropists also followed Owen's example at New Lanark and created model villages for their own workforces and improved conditions in their factories. Few were initially prepared like Owen to take the next step and entertain the possibility that working people could run co-operative or community businesses on their own terms, although in some cases a measure of community control was over time passed to the residents.

The search for alternatives to the social evils of Victorian and Edwardian England continued, and time and again a version of community business was at the heart of the attempt. There was the Guild socialism of John Ruskin, the farm colonies established by William Booth and George Lansbury, and the Garden City movement inspired by Ebenezer Howard.

In the years before the First World War the role of the state increased, with the establishment of municipal authorities in the great cities, and the 1908 Old Age Pensions Act was followed by the 1911 National Insurance Act which brought in a contributory social security system, providing rudimentary health care and unemployment benefit. But these measures proved inadequate to deal with the stock market crash of 1929 and the subsequent Great Depression. National unemployment more than doubled by 1930 and sometimes reached over 60% in the industrial districts, blighting large areas of Wales, northern England, Scotland and Northern Ireland.

In one of the worst affected areas in South Wales the Brynmawr Experiment, a community business initiated by Quakers, established a furniture business of such quality that it was able to open a retail outlet in the heart of London's West End.

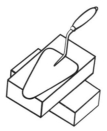

Building
societies

The first known building society was formed in 1775 by Richard Ketley, the landlord at the 'Golden Cross' inn at 60 Snow Hill in Birmingham. It was a form of friendly society, the members of which would each contribute a specified amount into a shared building fund and draw lots to select which of the members would have land purchased and a home constructed. With property in place as security, the plan was to attract further finance to the society through loans at a reasonable cost. In 1779 a newspaper advertisement claimed that £80 had been advanced on the society's shares.

This, like many others which followed across the Midlands and Northern England, were known as 'terminating' societies, meaning that they would be wound up when all their members had been housed. By 1825 there were already over 250 such societies in existence, and in 1836 the Regulation of Benefit Building Societies Act officially recognised building societies for the first time.

The co-operative movement was quick to see the opportunity and the potential benefit. In 1861 the Rochdale Pioneer Land and Building Company (later the Equitable Pioneer Society) provided co-operative housing on land in Spotland Road in Rochdale.

By 1867 it had built 84 homes, and the street names proudly proclaimed their co-operative origins: Equitable Street and Pioneer Street. By the end of the century the Society had built no less than 300 houses for rent.

A second wave of co-operative housing development came with the tenant co-partnership movement in the early 1900s. Starting in 1901 with the founding of Ealing Tenants Ltd, the first tenant co-partnership co-operative was built at Brentham Garden Suburb. The idea was to build houses that members would own collectively and rent themselves, so that 'every man would be his neighbour's landlord.'

By 1910 there were 1,723 building societies in existence with 626,000 members and total assets of over £76m.

The 1836 Act had also encouraged the formation of 'permanent' building societies, the first of which was the Metropolitan Equitable in 1845. This allowed investors to make deposits and receive interest on their savings, regardless of whether or not they wanted a house. The new model was successful in attracting private capital, allowing the societies to build up reserve funds, and vastly increase the volume of house-building. But on the other hand, the original principles of mutual aid were weakened, and the permanent building societies, while retaining a nominally social model, became less and less connected to local communities.

Commercial considerations led to mergers and acquisitions, and eventually to the formation of very large entities such as Abbey National, Cheltenham & Gloucester, and Halifax. A century and a half later the 1986 New Building Societies Act allowed them to convert to privately owned companies. Many society members, attracted by financial windfalls, voted for privatisation and some of the largest social businesses the country had ever seen disappeared for ever. But not all, and the Nationwide building society, with community origins in Ramsbury in Wiltshire in 1846 (the Provident Union Building Society) and Northampton in 1848 (the Town and County Freehold Land Society), now has ten million members. In 2016 it achieved £32bn of mortgage lending and profits of £1.3bn, and continues to be owned by its members rather than private shareholders.

The friendly society or co-operative model was not the only way to provide social housing as an alternative to the dreadful conditions of the Victorian slum. Wealthy philanthropists also got in on the act, establishing charitable trusts for the purpose.

The first was the Labourer's Friend Society founded by Lord Shaftesbury in 1830. It began by providing allotments of land to labourers for cottage husbandry, and in 1844 changed its name to the Society for Improving the Condition of the Labouring Classes, and established a 'Model Dwellings Company' to raise finance. However, the design of its first scheme at Pentonville was functional and utilitarian, and the estate was regarded as grim and unpleasant.

Others followed, including The Metropolitan Association for Improving the Dwellings of the Industrious Classes. Its purpose was to provide 'the labouring man with an increase of the comforts and conveniences of life, with full return to the capitalist.' A five per cent return was promised to investors, and the model soon acquired the label 'Five Percent Philanthropy'.

The first Peabody estates were opened in Spitalfields in 1864 and Islington in 1865, funded through a Trust set up by the American banker George Peabody. A square courtyard was surrounded by blocks of housing five storeys high, with shared laundries on the top floor. Railings separated the estate from the surrounding streets, and the gates were closed at 11pm each night. The flats were not self-contained, and there were shared sinks and lavatories on the landings, in a style known as 'associated dwellings', enabling the facilities to be inspected regularly for cleanliness.

In 1871 the wealthy art critic and philanthropist John Ruskin established the St. George's Fund to finance the acquisition of land for affordable housing in villages and to help protect and revive rural industries and crafts. Ruskin also provided finance to Octavia Hill, to help her establish her first housing scheme in Marylebone in 1871, to provide homes to be rented out to the labouring classes. Octavia Hill employed women to collect rent on a weekly basis to reduce the risk of arrears, but also to get to know tenants personally and encourage them to better themselves. It was an early form of social work.

In 1890, philanthropist Sir Edward Cecil Guinness, the great grandson of the founder of the Guinness Brewery, gave £200,000 to set up the Guinness Trust. In the first eleven years eight tenement estates were built, providing over 2,500 homes. They were designed with 'health, morality and social stability' in mind: glazed bricks and tiles were used to prevent disease spreading and tenants were expected to scrub the corridors and their own quarters, and presumably themselves, frequently.

These early trusts gave birth to the housing association movement. Many of these early housing associations survive to the present day, and have played an important and enduring role in improving the quality of housing for working people. But the role of private philanthropy gradually fell away, particularly with the rise of municipal council housing in the 1920s and 1930s. As we shall see, housing associations were later established by immigrant communities and others working in deprived neighbourhoods as an expression of community self-determination and self-help. But from the 1980s onwards housing associations became increasingly regarded as an instrument of public policy by successive governments, and as with building societies, the desire to attract greater levels of commercial investment led to consolidation and regulation and a loss of community connection, as the state and the market stepped in. It is only in the most recent years that we have started to see a revival of independent community-led housing, in the form of community land trusts and similar models, and we will return to this in later chapters.

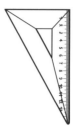

Model communities

In 1830 Thomas Bazley and Richard Gardner bought and demolished a mill at Barrow Bridge near Bolton, replacing it with Dean Mills, and in 1831 created a model village for the mill workers on a hill accessed by a flight of stone steps, with rows of cottages, a shop and an educational institute. A canteen was provided for the workforce, hot water for tea and coffee, and hot baths and showers. The factory ovens baked 150 loaves a day for the workers.

Benjamin Disraeli visited the village in 1840, and it became the basis of the fictional village Millbank in his novel, Coningsby, published in 1844, where it is described in idyllic terms:

> 'A village of not inconsiderable size, and remarkable from the neatness and even picturesque character of its architecture, and the gay gardens that surrounded it. On a sunny knoll in the background rose a church, in the best style of Christian architecture, and near it was a clerical residence and a school-house of similar design. The village, too, could boast of another public building; an Institute where there were a library and a lecture-room; and a reading-hall, which any one might frequent at certain hours, and under reasonable regulations.'

This was not to be an isolated example. A succession of commercially astute and philanthropically-minded industrialists went on to build model settlements for their workforces. From Bessbrook, in Northern Ireland, to Akroyden near Halifax and Bromborough Pool on the Wirral, philanthropic industrialists built model settlements for their workforces with the aim of improving their health, living conditions, and often also their morals.

One of the finest of all model villages was Saltaire, named after its founder Titus Salt, on the outskirts of Bradford. In the first fifty years of the 19th century, as the industrial revolution gathered pace, the population of Bradford grew from 13,000 to over 100,000. There, in 1833, Titus Salt took over a textile company set up by his father. The company prospered, and Titus proved to be a shrewd and energetic entrepreneur. One day he noticed 300 bales of wool gathering dust in a Liverpool warehouse. It was alpaca wool from Peru and nobody had any use for it, so Salt took a sample and, in great secrecy, experimented with the fibres, producing a type of worsted cloth. He bought the bales up cheap, and the cloth he manufactured took Victorian high fashion by storm. His fortune was made, and Titus Salt became the biggest employer in Bradford.

With over 200 factory chimneys belching smoke, Bradford was at this time the most polluted town in England. Sewage was dumped into the river where people obtained their drinking water and there were regular outbreaks of cholera and typhoid. Only 30% of working class children born to textile workers reached the age of 15, and average life expectancy was just over 18 years.

Titus Salt was one of the few employers in the town who showed much concern, and in 1842 he installed in all his factories a new type of smoke burner which dramatically reduced pollution. In 1848 he became mayor of Bradford and tried to persuade the council to pass a by-law that would force all mills in the town to use the new smoke burners, but he was met with determined opposition: the other mill-owners refused to admit any connection between the smoke from their chimneys and the deaths of the children.

In disgust, Salt decided to move out of Bradford. In 1850 he announced plans to build a new industrial community three miles outside Bradford in healthy countryside on the banks of the River Aire. There were good commercial reasons for this: he would have an improved water supply, he would be able to install modern machinery, and he would have a healthier and therefore more productive workforce.

Titus Salt named his new village Saltaire, and it took twenty years to build. At the centre of the village was the mill, which contained the largest single room in the Western world at the time. At the grand opening of the mill in 1853, 3,500 guests ate two tons of meat, half a ton of potatoes, 320 plum puddings and 100 jellies.

At first, the 3,500 workers had to travel from their homes in Bradford to work in Saltaire. However, during the next few years, 850 houses were built. There were semi-detached houses for the managers, while ordinary workman had cottages with a living room, scullery and three bedrooms, far superior to those available to working people elsewhere. Fresh water was piped into each home from Saltaire's own reservoir, and gas was laid on to provide lighting and heating. Unlike the people of Bradford, every family in Saltaire had its own outside lavatory.

To encourage people to keep themselves clean, Salt also built public baths and wash-houses. Saltaire had its own church, school, hospital, library and a variety of shops. Forty-five almshouses were provided rent free with a pension of ten shillings a week to retired persons of 'good moral character'. Salt decreed that there would be no public house, no pawn shop and no police station. A notice at the entrance of the village said 'Abandon beer all ye who enter here,' although in 1867 an off-licence was allowed in the village. The mill's security officer had a house on a street corner with a glass windowed tower on the roof so that, it was said, he could observe the activities of the villagers.

In 1870 a club and institute were opened, and Salt declared to the villagers: 'It is intended to supply the advantages of a public house without its evils; it will be a place to which you can resort for conversation, business, recreation and refreshment, as well as for education – elementary, technical and scientific.' Salt also provided a park, and altered the course of the river Aire to improve the view and allow boating, but smoking, gambling and swearing were banned. Numerous societies were established under Salt's patronage, the most popular being the Horticultural, Pig, Dog, Poultry and Pigeon Society. Charles Dickens visited in 1857 and reported that 'all looked prosperous and happy.' In 1874 *Practical Magazine* described the town as 'a nation in miniature, a little kingdom within a kingdom'.

Salt supported adult suffrage and in 1835 he was a founder of the Bradford Reform Association. He publicly supported the Chartists and condemned the 1832 Reform Act with which the government attempted to buy off Chartist demands for universal suffrage. Salt was a strong advocate of profit sharing, although unable to carry his partners on this point. But he was certainly no soft touch; he employed child labour, and opposed legislation raising from eight to ten the age at which children could be employed in factories as 'half-timers'. He was not sympathetic to trade unions and in 1876 unrest in his mill was met with a lock-out of all workers.

Although he had been an extremely rich man, when Salt died in 1876 his fortune was gone. His family was horrified to discover that during his life he had given away over £500,000 to good causes.

Another celebrated Victorian philanthropist was George Cadbury, who had made a fortune in the chocolate business. The success of his company stemmed from a decision in 1866 to produce cocoa powder which, unlike that produced by their competitors, was unadulterated. Cadbury's market position was reinforced by legislation passed in 1875 which prevented manufacturers from labelling adulterated cocoa as pure cocoa.

In 1878 Cadbury built a model community on fourteen and a half acres of land near the stream of Bourne, south west of Birmingham. He named it Bourneville, a name chosen to help the company compete with rival French chocolate makers. At Bourneville, Cadbury provided housing, cricket and football pitches, open air swimming pools, and a full-sized concert hall and lecture theatre.

Bourneville became known as the factory in the garden. Cadbury said that 'no man ought to be compelled to live where a rose cannot grow.' A tenth of the estate was reserved for public open space, and public buildings, shops and schools were built round a large common. Every residence had a large garden laid out with vegetable patches, flower beds and fruit trees. The value of garden produce was estimated as equivalent to a saving of two shillings a week on the rents for householders, and Cadbury's proud boast was that the villagers grew £58 of food per acre where before the same land had yielded only £5 per acre.

As with Titus Salt at Saltaire, corridors were arranged to keep boys and girls separate on their way to or from work, and they had separate recreation areas on either side of the main road. Cottages provided for female employees were protected by night watchmen, one of whose duties was to light fires in the afternoon so that the women came home to a warm home in the evening. But Cadbury refused to employ married women, believing that a wife's place was in the home.

Originally Cadbury wanted owner occupiers, but several who bought on advantageous terms sold at a profit so Cadbury vested all the property in the Bourneville Village Trust. He insisted that the Trust made 5% profit, on the Five Percent Philanthropy model, to prove that such a venture was not bound to make a loss. A democratically elected council was set up to run some aspects of the village affairs and as a consultative body. In all of this he inspired his friend, business rival, and fellow Quaker Joseph Rowntree, and the later Garden City movement.

Cadbury had no time for those who kept their business and

philanthropic interests separate. He believed that it was just as important that money should be made rightly as that it should be spent rightly. By 1919, the Cadbury's company was the largest chocolate manufacturer in the world and had a system of elected works councils on which the 7,500 employees and the management were given equal representation.

In 1887 William Hesketh Lever, the 'soap king', bought 56 acres of land in the Wirral and building work started on his Port Sunlight soap factory and village. Lever's aims were 'to socialise and Christianise business relations and get back to the office, factory and workshop that close family brotherhood that existed in the good old days of hand labour.'

Between 1899 and 1914, 800 houses with a population of 3,500 were built at Port Sunlight, together with a generous supply of allotments and public buildings. At the opening of the recreation and dining hall for men, the Prime Minister Gladstone declared 'In this hall I have found living proof that cash payment is not the only nexus between man and man.'

In 1922 Lever opened an art gallery, in memory of his wife. Other facilities included a cottage hospital, schools, a concert hall, open air swimming pool, church, and a temperance hotel. Two years after the hotel opened a referendum showed that 80% of villagers wanted it to sell intoxicating drinks and Lever reluctantly bowed to the wishes of the majority. It was a healthy community by the standards of the day: in the early 1900s infant mortality in Port Sunlight was 70 per 1,000 compared to 140 per 1,000 in nearby Liverpool.

Lever claimed that Port Sunlight was an exercise in 'profit sharing'. But rather than share profits with the workers directly, he invested them in the village, as he explained in his most patronising manner: 'It would not do you much good if you send it down your throats in the form of bottles of whisky, bags of sweets, or fat geese at Christmas. On the other hand, if you leave the money with me, I shall use it to provide for you everything that makes life pleasant – viz nice houses, comfortable homes, and healthy recreation.' Of course, many community businesses today take a similar approach, but there is one difference: the decision to do is taken by a community Board rather than by a wealthy benefactor.

However, over time, the ownership and control of the Port Sunlight recreation and dining hall transferred to local people. Since 1993 it has been run as a theatre by the Gladstone Theatre Trust. It holds an annual Drama Festival, and is used by local operatic societies, musical groups, youth organisations, and dancing schools.

In 1869 Joseph Rowntree, the son of a grocer, went into partnership with his brother Henry who owned the 'Cocoa, Chocolate & Chicory Works' in York. On the death of Henry in 1883, Joseph became the sole owner, and with the help of products such as fruit pastilles, chocolate drops, fruit gums and jelly babies he turned a small company into a thriving international enterprise, employing 4,000 people by the turn of the century.

Joseph Rowntree was a Quaker and was determined to understand the causes of poverty and do what he could to address them and alleviate the effects, publishing a study on the subject, *Pauperism in England and Wales*, in 1865. His son Benjamin Seebohm Rowntree followed in the footsteps of his father and carried out a landmark investigation into poverty in York, published in 1901 as *Poverty, A Study of Town Life*.

Influenced by this research, and by his Quaker principles, Joseph took measures to improve the quality of life of his own employees. He provided a library and free education for workers under seventeen, and employed a social welfare officer, doctor and dentist in his factory. He donated £10,000 to establish a workers' pension fund, and gave the workers a say in the appointment of their immediate supervisors.

In 1901 Joseph Rowntree purchased 123 acres at New Earswick on the edge of York to build houses for his employees and other working people. The planner Raymond Unwin and the architect Barry Parker were commissioned to produce an overall plan for a new 'garden' village, influenced by the success of George Cadbury's Bourneville, and by the ideas of Ebenezer Howard. The houses at New Earswick were of a good quality and had gardens with fruit trees and enough land to grow vegetables. At least one tenth of the land was to be reserved for parks and other green spaces.

A Trust was established, controlled by the Rowntree family, and the Trust Deed enshrined its social mission: 'Nothing may be done under the powers hereby conferred which may prevent the growth of civic interest, and a sense of civic responsibility, amongst those who may live in any community existing on the property of the Trust.' The principles of housing management were inspired by Octavia Hill. Rent collection, problems of arrears, care of property, selection and transfer of tenants, welfare and the proper introduction of tenants into a new community were placed in the hands of one person. Prospective tenants were carefully selected, and later it was acknowledged that 'families apparently incapable of maintaining a satisfactory home' were kept away, thus avoiding 'the social problems which often hamper the growth of community life in publicly-provided estates.'

Rowntree donated a splendid Folk Hall, and at its opening he remarked, 'It is often said that Village life is dull, and so I fear it generally is, but there is no occasion for its being so.' He hoped the hall would be used for religious services, an adult school, billiards, 'popular Lectures with the Magic Lantern', musical gatherings, debating or literary societies, photographic exhibitions, exhibitions of a horticultural society, political meetings. It became the 'Village Club', and so was an early example of the multi-use community centre which was later to be found in many communities across the country.

Joseph Rowntree hoped that New Earswick would become a self-governing community. He wrote in a private memorandum: 'I do not want to establish communities bearing the stamp of charity but rather of rightly ordered and self-governing communities – self-governing, that is, within the broad limits laid down by the Trust.' He recognised the difficulties of community decision-making but did not regard them as insuperable: 'Man is a somewhat quarrelsome animal, and it requires some thought and wisdom for companies of persons to work harmoniously together. Most of us have to learn how to give and take, and to know how far it is wise and right to press our own views. If a meeting or a committee comes to a pretty united decision which we think to be mistaken, it may yet often be the right course for us to accept such decision and to do our best to make it work smoothly.'

The Village Council first met in 1904. It discussed 'everything from the name of the growing village to the problem of overflowing rain butts.' Rowntree promised that it would be 'thoroughly democratic' and be able to take responsibility rather than wait for initiative from the trustees of the Trust. However, it turned out that the Village Council was to be little more than a consultative body, only able to recommend improvements to the community assets it managed rather than to exert control.

Moreover, the income the Village Council received from the Folk Hall was only just sufficient to meet running costs. The building had been provided free and the Trust was responsible for repairs and redecoration. 'However sincere the efforts to avoid paternalism, it must remain true that the community life of the village is thus largely dependent either directly or indirectly on money provided by the Trust.' There were attempts to avoid a sense of dependency. In 1935 the villagers asked the Trust to extend the Folk Hall. As with many funders today, the Trust wanted first to be assured that the residents would contribute 'in some small measure' to the cost.' The residents contributed £500, an impressive amount at that time.

In 1942 Seebohm Rowntree felt able to declare that the aims of the model village had been achieved and that in particular there was 'a strong feeling of communal responsibility among those living there.' That may have been true, but the larger object of achieving a self-determining community had never been fully realised.

In 1925 Dorothy and Leonard Elmhirst purchased the neglected 14th century Dartington estate outside Totnes in Devon. With their vast personal wealth they were able to restore the estate buildings and set up a host of farming, forestry and educational projects. The 'Dartington Experiment' became a magnet for artists, architects, writers, philosophers and musicians from around the world.

Early initiatives included Dartington Hall School, Dartington Tweed Mill and later Dartington Glass. In 1977 the Cider Press Centre opened as a retail centre selling local crafts and other products and continues to this day to trade successfully, as The Shops at Dartington. In 1991, the White Hart Bar and Restaurant and the Dartington Conference Centre opened.

Today the Dartington Hall Trust continues to operate as a social enterprise, with shops, a cinema, a restaurant and café, visitor accommodation, and camping facilities. It also hosts a regional school for start-up social ventures, in partnership with the School for Social Entrepreneurs. Widely admired, both nationally and internationally, Dartington Hall's relationship with its community was not always been a happy one. It remained essentially a philanthropic venture, with little scope for its local community to set the direction or exercise ownership or control. However, in recent times there have been renewed attempts to rediscover the ambition of its founders that Dartington should become 'a place where living and learning could flourish together and where the practical life was balanced with the activities of the mind and the spirit' and to reanimate its local community connections.

And perhaps it is no accident that neighbouring Totnes has become fertile territory for imaginative community-led action. It is the home of the worldwide Transition Towns movement, which has pioneered community led action to tackle climate change. And in 2016 a local referendum produced an 86% vote in favour of a community takeover of a derelict industrial site in Totnes in order to provide 62 affordable homes, a health and well-being centre, and workspaces offering 160 jobs in local businesses - in effect a modern-day model village run by its community as a community business.

Unlike the self-organising co-operative communities, or O'Conner's chartist Land Plan, the actions of wealthy philanthropists were not threatening to the status quo, and Parliament was happy enough for them to build model villages for people employed in their factories.

They were much admired, though occasionally mocked for their high moral tone. They had excellent schools, and recreational institutions designed to stimulate self-improvement. Most maintained a ban on alcohol, and introduced rules to prevent disorderly behaviour, which in the case of Saltaire including a ban on hanging washing out on a line.

In the early days of these communities, local residents had little if any ownership and control, and there was little or no encouragement by the founding philanthropists to set up community-run businesses. But over time, as we have seen, there were tentative efforts to transfer some measure of control to residents, and to establish entrepreneurial ventures which could be run by and provide benefit for the community.

Darkest England and the way out

In 1871 the wealthy art critic and philanthropist John Ruskin founded the Guild of St George. He wanted to demonstrate an alternative to the industrial system, by promoting traditional crafts based within rural communes. This was to be achieved through a resurrection, in a highly idealised form, of the medieval guild system.

Land would be purchased for labourers, allowing them to be taken out of the workhouses and work 'under the carefullest supervision and with every proper means of mental instruction.' Every trade and profession would have its own costume. The new order would flourish on a European scale, with a hierarchy led by a supreme Master, a post which Ruskin himself would reluctantly hold, but only until someone more suitable could be found. The supreme Master would preside over provincial Marshals, and local Landlords, and below them, at the bottom of the pile, the Labourers. This edifice would be supported financially by Companions who would voluntarily give a tenth of their wages to the Guild. Ruskin promoted his plan as a form of socialism, but it was a far cry from the co-operative or mutual aid model where working people themselves were able to exercise ownership and control.

Perhaps surprisingly, this scheme attracted supporters. Donations of land from wealthy Companions eventually placed land and properties in the Guild's care: Wyre Forest near Bewdley,

Worcestershire, Barmouth in Gwynedd, north-west Wales; Cloughton in North Yorkshire, and Westmill in Hertfordshire. In 1876 Ruskin purchased a thirteen-acre estate at Totley near Sheffield to form a community of working men, and this became known as St George's Farm. Ruskin hoped the community would develop a spiritual character, 'more in the spirit of a body of monks gathered for missionary service, than of a body of tradesmen gathered for the promotion even of the honestest and usefullest trade.'

The community at Totley was mainly composed of shoemakers, and Ruskin expected that they would be able to raise their standard of craftsmanship and, he promised, would also be allowed to experiment with a suitable form of self-government. But from the start there were tensions. The community was in fact to be governed not by the shoemakers but by William Harrison Riley, who proclaimed himself a Christian Socialist, and declared that 'it is the duty of all able-bodied persons to earn their own living by their own labour.' He also believed that 'the land of Great Britain is the national inheritance of the Commonwealth' and that all buildings, crops and produce of the land should 'be used for the good of the Commonwealth.' Food, fuel clothing and other materials necessary for human life should be distributed to all citizens according to their needs, and 'all citizens should have a right to do as they please, providing that they do not threaten or interfere with the rights of other people.'

The Sheffield shoemakers had other ideas. They wanted to become residents in the community rather than daily travellers to it. They fell into dispute with Riley who finally emigrated to the United States. Attempts were then made to produce strawberries, currants and gooseberries on the farm, and the colony survived for ten years. Ruskin blamed the eventual failure of the experiment on the poor quality of the land, but poor management and a lack of community ownership was perhaps a more likely cause. Ruskin eventually sold the land to a socialist farmer George Pearson and the family nursery business he founded continues to this day.

On the Isle of Man the Guild invested in St George's Mill, a spinning and handloom weaving mill, established by a local weaver Egbert Rydings in 1877. It promoted traditional crafts and provided employment for local people, and was described at the time as a 'sort of hospice for the poor widows, orphans, deaf and dumb, and cripples in the parish.' It struggled financially, but lasted until 1901, when the mill was sold privately and the loan made by the Guild was repaid.

In the United States Julius Wayland sought to apply Ruskin's ideas on a larger scale. He published a newspaper The Coming Nation which attracted 50,000 subscribers and went on to purchase 1,000 acres near Tennessee City, where he established the town of Ruskin with a school, bakery, café, steam laundry, and cannery as well as workshops which produced household goods such as suspenders, leather belts, 'Ruskin chewing gum' and a patent medicine called 'Ruskin Ready Remedy'. By 1897 the town of Ruskin had 250 inhabitants, but arguments over voting rights for wives of new members led to the break-up of the colony in 1899.

In 1888 Charles Robert Ashbee, a leading proponent of the Arts and Craft movement, inspired in part by Ruskin, established the Guild and School of Handicrafts while living at the East London university settlement Toynbee Hall. He soon moved out to larger premises at Essex House in Whitechapel, where the Guild produced jewellery and enamels, hand-wrought copper and wrought ironwork, as well as furniture and decorative painting. In 1901 the Guild then moved to Chipping Campden in the Cotswolds. However the local market for craftsman-designed furniture and metalwork was soon saturated and there was growing competition from machine-made replicas sold by shops such as Heals and Liberty's. The Guild was liquidated in 1907. A friend of Ashbee, Godfrey Blount, set up Haslemere Peasant Industries in 1896 in Surrey, with the intention of enjoying 'the double pleasure of lovely surroundings and happy work.' Under the umbrella of this organisation small craft workshops were established, reviving local craft traditions notably weaving and embroidery as well as ironwork, pottery, woodwork, fresco painting, hand-press printing, bookbinding, plasterwork and carving. Most of the workshops came to an end during the First World War.

Prince Peter Kropotkin, the Russian anarchist, visited England in 1876, again in 1881, and then from 1886 he lived much of the time in London and in Brighton. True society, Kropotkin asserted, would be restored by establishing free village communities. In response to Social Darwinism with its insistence on the survival of the fittest, Kropotkin published a series of articles, including 'The Coming Reign of Plenty' and 'The Industrial Village of the Future', showing how the guilds and free communes of medieval Europe afforded examples of freely co-operating non-political institutions. In 1892 he reprinted these articles in book form as *Conquete du Pain* (translated in 1906 as *The Conquest of Bread*). Here and elsewhere he argued for 'a society without a state', a federation of free communes.

An anarchist colony at Norton Hall near Sheffield was set up by followers of the socialist Edward Carpenter, much influenced by Kropotkin's ideas. The colonists were teetotal, vegetarian, non-smoking, grew lettuce and manufactured sandals. A further attempt to test the theories propounded by Kropotkin took place at Clousden Hill near Newcastle. Here in 1895 four men, two with small families, took a farm consisting of 20 acres of poor land. They pooled their money into a common fund, there were no wages, and each received pocket money according to how the fund stood. Eating was communal. They sold produce to the Sunderland and Newcastle Co-operatives and traded with the Newcastle Green market. The settlement was visited by the trade unionist Tom Mann, Kropotkin himself, and others, and kept going until the turn of the century.

Count Leo Tolstoy, the Russian novelist and philosopher, rejected the modern state and all efforts to organise the external condition of peoples' lives, which he believed were a divergence from the inner needs of mankind. He called for an organic society based on self-government and co-operation of free men working in federated groups: small communities with as close a connection to nature as possible, based on a form of Christianity purged of dogmas and mysticism, 'not promising future bliss, but giving bliss on earth.'

In 1894 his followers established the Brotherhood Trust and set up a grocery and vegetable co-operative in Downham Rd, Kingsland, in North London. All the profits including the customer dividend were to be used to purchase land to establish communities. In 1897 a community was indeed established at Purleigh on a twenty-three-acre estate, with fruit trees and a kitchen garden, and a printing press. It foundered over debates about whether or not to admit homeless vagrants, and internal dissension was compounded by the mental instability of some of its leaders. Other communities were formed in Essex, Leeds, and Blackburn, and also at Leicester where in Braunstone in 1899 five vegetarians acquired half an acre of land and formed a land society to acquire more.

Another Tolstoyan colony near Stroud at Whiteway survives to this day. Founded in 1898, there was to be no ownership of land, no currency, no forces of law and order, no taxes and no government. Only the initial purchase of 42 acres of countryside involved cash. After that they burned the property deeds on the end of a pitchfork. All would be held in common, and the colonists would live on what they could grow. Later, some of the colonists began to sell their produce, and the Cotswold Co-operative Handicrafts Guild was formed, selling cloth, sandals and wooden craftwork. In 1926 Ibrahim Ismail from Somaliland joined the leather workers and was taught the craft of bookbinding. The members agreed to divide the sales money by the combined hours worked, and so the rate was set for all, everyone being treated equally.

In 1865 William Booth founded an evangelical Christian mission in the east End of London, which later developed into the Salvation

Army. In 1890 he established his first 'Elevator' in Whitechapel, which was a combination of workshop and hostel accommodation, designed to help destitute people acquire skills and pay their way for their board and lodging. The trades practised in the Salvation Army Elevators included basket-making and brush-making, carpentry, joinery and cabinet making, French polishing, carpet weaving, and tailoring as well as recycling of household salvage, especially waste paper. A salvage wharf was set up on the Thames at Battersea, where waste paper, tin cans and old clothes were collected and recycled, and a giant riverside sign advertised its presence: 'Darkest England Salvage Convertor'.

The Salvation Army was criticised for paying wages lower than prevailing trade union rates, and wages at the Elevators were paid in part by tokens which could only be spent at approved stores, where alcohol was not sold. But in 1891 Booth opened a match factory at Bow in East London, paying wages which were higher than the industry average, and manufacturing the new safety matches which he advertised as 'Lights in Darkest England'. The venture was intended to demonstrate the alternative to other match factories where wages were extremely low and where the use of phosphorous caused necrosis of facial bones ('phossy jaw') among the workforce.

In 1890 Booth set out his plans for social reform in an influential book, *Darkest England and the Way Out*. He proposed that the 'submerged tenth' of the urban population could be rescued by progression from urban hostels to farm colonies, and from there to a new life in the colonies overseas. In 1891 he purchased 3,000 acres of farmland at Hadleigh in Essex. Already by the end of the first year, temporary dwellings had been erected, including five dormitories, a dining room, kitchen, bathroom, offices, a reading room and meeting room, and a sixteen-bed hospital. As well as farming, brickworks were established, producing bricks for the colony's own housing, and a railway was laid down so that the bricks could be transported to the estuary and ferried along the Thames to London. It was a large scale enterprise: by the end of 1892, the production rate was 150,000 bricks per week.

A booklet produced in 1902 explained that the objective of the Colony was to give employment and food and lodging in return for labour, to any able-bodied man who was willing to work, 'irrespective of nationality or creed'. However, everyone was expected to attend religious services at the 'Citadel' on a Sunday, and when attendance proved disappointing a roll-call was made to enforce the practice.

There was to be no alcohol. Newcomers started off as a lower class of resident, and were rewarded if they improved themselves by rising into a higher class, with better dormitory accommodation and better food. During the 1890s there were 250 colonists at work and in 1906 Booth launched a second project, also in Essex, where a separate house was built for each plot. If a tenant passed a two year probationary period, they would be offered a 999 year lease. By the 1920s as many as 1,000 people a year from the slums of the East End were being trained in the farm colonies and made ready to emigrate to a life overseas.

General Booth rejected the co-operative model absolutely. He was in favour of 'the directing brain' rather than any notion of democratic government, which he derided as 'the principle of counting noses'. Moreover, he required 'universal and unquestioning obedience from those at the bottom'. From a political point of view Booth was a die-hard conservative. But the idea of establishing farm colonies as a means to 'elevate' the lives of impoverished East Enders was also taken up by one of the most celebrated socialists of the day, George Lansbury.

In 1892 Lansbury, who was later to become MP for Bow and Bromley, Mayor of Poplar, and eventually leader of the Labour party, became a member of the Board of Guardians of the Poplar Workhouse. He soon began a policy of relief beyond the workhouse, and with support from Joseph Fels, an American philanthropist, established two 'colonies' at Laindon in Essex and Hollesley Bay in Suffolk. As with the farm colonies set up by General Booth, the aim was to settle unemployed Londoners. Most came from the workhouse, and many were former soldiers. A hundred men were housed in corrugated iron huts and set to digging reservoirs and building chicken huts. The plan was to turn the site into co-operative smallholdings, but the Local Government Board refused to allow this.

Encouraged by the experiments at Laindon and Hollesley Bay, Joseph Fels went on to purchase a 600-acre farm at Mayland in Essex, applying intensive horticultural principles developed by Thomas Smith, who had already established a small socialist colony nearby.

In 1898 Ebenezer Howard, an obscure court stenographer, published *Tomorrow: A Peaceful Plan to Real Reform*. This book set out a vision of a garden city of 30,000 people on a 6,000 acre estate, intended to combine the very best of town and country life.

The Garden City Association was formed in 1899, and its members visited and admired experiments at Port Sunlight and Bourneville. In September 1903 the 'First Garden City Ltd' was incorporated and construction began at Letchworth, on 3,800 acres costing £160,000. Schools were established on advanced principles: the school diet was based on butter, milk, eggs, fresh fruit, and vegetables, and morning assemblies were deliberative rather than devotional. Letchworth attracted a stream of people keen to discover new ways of living: Tolstoyans, anarchists, vegetarians, trade unionists, socialists, followers of Ruskin, and even Lenin, who found refuge there for a short time in 1907. George Orwell was to say that in the garden city you could find 'every fruit juice drinker, sandal wearer, sex maniac, Quaker, nature cure quack, pacifist and feminist in England.'

Howard's approach was distinguished by its treatment of land values and tenure arrangements. Land for the settlement would be purchased by a Trust at agricultural land values with a rate of return for investors of not more than 4%. All occupants would pay a rent and the income received in this way would be used to pay capital with interest to investors, and to pay for the general running costs and welfare of the garden city. Income for the latter purpose would increase as the former fell away. This was a radically different model from that which applied elsewhere, where rising land values were enjoyed simply as a source of profit for private landlords. The secret, claimed Howard, was to retain the land in common ownership and to build this into the plan from the outset.

The influence of Letchworth spread rapidly. Joseph Rowntree appointed Raymond Unwin, the gifted architect of Letchworth, to design his New Earswick settlement outside York. Hampstead Garden Suburb was begun in 1907. A Garden Cities Association was set up and grew into the Town and Country Planning Association; the first Town Planning Act came into force in 1909 to regulate development.

In 1920, Ebenezer Howard, together with a group of followers (including several Quakers) established Welwyn Garden City, with capital of a quarter of a million pounds. An agricultural guild was set up to supply the inhabitants of Welwyn with milk and vegetables, using land leased from the Garden City Company. The business was kept separate from the Trust, but without ownership of the land it had nothing to fall back on in time of financial difficulty. As a result it failed during the agricultural depression in the 1920s, and the land was re-let to tenant farmers.

In subsequent developments Howard's principles were much diluted. In the 1920s in Manchester the local authority purchased land and built Wythenshawe but this was little more than a sprawling estate with no town centre or community identity. In the 1930s, trading estates were established at Treforest in Glamorgan, Team Valley at Durham and Tyneside, and Hillington near Glasgow with large scale government investment, but these too were functional and uninspired places, and had little in common with Howard's original vision. After the Second World War, the garden city movement was revived in a succession of new towns, including Milton Keynes and Stevenage, and while design and facilities were generally of a higher standard, there were few opportunities for community ownership and control and for community business to flourish.

More recently, as we shall see, the community land trust model represents in many ways a revival of the original garden city idea, and has attracted a great deal of interest. Moreover, in 2014 the Letchworth Declaration called for improved accreditation of future garden cities and attempted to reinforce the principles of community ownership and control. This came at a time of renewed government interest in the garden city model, which was seen as a means to improve the supply of mixed-community housing while overcoming local opposition to large-scale housing development. In 2017 plans were announced to establish a series of garden villages and towns, although the extent to which these will create the conditions for entrepreneurial community-controlled initiative is yet to be seen.

As we have seen, these community experiments, driven by the urgent need to seek alternatives to the dreadful conditions of the industrial poor in the vast cities of late Victorian Britain, came from the left and the right of the political spectrum. In some cases they were autocratic in design, and in other cases informed by a radical democratic impulse, but all were founded on the belief that human dignity could be enhanced by replacing an inhumane factory system with craft-based forms of labour, simpler forms of production and consumption, and communities organised on a human scale. Some of these late Victorian and early Edwardian social reformers looked back to a mythical pre-industrial age of 'Merrie England', and for this they were often mocked by their contemporaries, and frequently derided as 'cranks'. But nevertheless they can now been seen, despite their occasional eccentricities, as anticipators of a yet-to-be-realised future where environmental and economic sustainability, a creative and useful life, and the building of community, count for more than the relentless accumulation of wealth at any price.

In times of trouble

Few places suffered more in the Great Depression of the late 1920s and early 1930s than Brynmawr in South Wales. The closure of collieries had devastated the local economy, and poverty was severe by any standards: gardens and allotments were abandoned for lack of seeds, pets were given up for lack of food, public services were reduced to a minimum, and shops closed down because customers were unable to pay for their goods. Hunger marchers took to the road to Newport. The town of Brynmawr was slowly starving. Then began the Brynmwar Experiment. It was to be the first of a long series of community businesses which have emerged in places experiencing catastrophic industrial decline.

In response to the national emergency and in particular to help the people of Brynmawr, a branch of the Quakers in Worthing set up a Coalfields Distress Committee. Their plan was to alleviate unemployment by developing light industry, and in 1929 a Quaker couple, Peter and Lillian Scott, believing that work should be controlled by the hands of those engaged in it, began the Brynmawr Experiment.

A community council was set up in Brynmawr to direct activities, and a community survey was undertaken. Local labour was organised to build an open air lido, with local men giving their service in exchange for a midday meal. The cost of the lido was £1,550 for materials and £600 for the food, but the scheme proved very popular and by charging a four pence entrance fee for swimmers and two pence for onlookers most of the cost was quickly recouped. It was an early example of a successful community-run swimming pool which many today might seek to emulate. Subsequently a nursery school was built in the same way, and a Subsistence Production Society was established to supply seeds and manure for allotments.

Some of the most malnourished children were housed with families in Worthing for a few months to help them recuperate. Sympathisers in Worthing raised £1,600 for a distress fund. A building was taken over as a Community House and became the base for welfare and social activities including a citizen's advice bureau and over twenty different youth clubs.

In 1931 Brynmawr and Clydach Valley Industries Limited was formed to create and manage local enterprises and provide work. An appeal was made with the aim of raising £15,000, and by July 1932, £10,579 had been collected: £5,672 in donations, £3,382 in shares, and £1,525 in loans. Further capital for new companies was raised by issuing shares to the workers in the form of loans from the umbrella group. Surpluses produced by the companies would repay the loans and control of the company would end up in the hands of the shareholders, the workers themselves.

Various enterprises were attempted. A weaving venture employed some two dozen women, making long stockings for farmers and colliers, and quilts of silk filled with wool, but this only lasted for two years. But another, Brynmawr Bootmakers, was successful throughout the 1930s, winning army contracts during the Second World War, and becoming fully self-financing.

The most celebrated of the Brynmawr community businesses was the Brynmawr Furniture Makers which began production in 1931 at a converted brewery, Gwalia Works. The furniture was designed by the talented Paul Matt on minimalist Arts and Craft principles and quickly established a nationwide reputation. Peter Scott and Paul Matt set out their ideals: 'We believe that to be of good design an article must be supremely fit for purpose: the materials employed must express their natural qualities: a balanced harmony of line, colour and texture must be achieved.'

An order was placed for 250 chairs for a Quaker boarding school in York, soon followed by another for 150 chairs for a community hall on a council estate in Birmingham, and so the business was up and running. At its height around fifty people were employed. While working conditions were basic, as in many other cases before and after the successful establishment of the community business was accompanied by a revival of associative life. According to a Brynmawr Bulletin produced in 1933 the workforce was 'notorious for their vocal versatility during working hours,' and an amateur operatic society was set up, as well as a flourishing sports club.

Marketing of the Brynmawr furniture was undertaken on the most advanced principles, through newspaper articles, promotional leaflets, Art Deco posters, a glossy catalogue entitled *Designed for the Modern Home*, and two specially commissioned promotional films. Exhibitions of the furniture were held in Liverpool, Cardiff, Birmingham, Manchester, London and elsewhere. In May 1938 a showroom opened in London's fashionable Cavendish Square.

The company was successfully selling its message of product excellence and social value. Only the Second World War brought a halt to this thriving community business, as it became impossible to import materials, and employees were conscripted into the army or into a nearby ammunition factory. The stock and equipment were sold and the company closed. A month after the closure the government issued an invitation to the Brynmawr Furniture Makers to produce 'Utility' furniture for those who had lost homes in the bombing, but sadly the invitation had come too late to save the business.

Encouraged by the results at Brynmawr, the government supported a rapid expansion of the Subsistence Production Society from 1934 to 1938. In the Welsh valleys hundreds of acres were acquired at Llandegveth, Beili Glas, Trevethin, Pontymoile, Griffithstown, Pontnewydd, Cwnbran and Cwnavon. In Lancashire sites were established at Billinge, Parbold Hall, Pemberton and Standish, supported by a grant of £30,000 from the Nuffield Trust. Commercial activities ranged from animal husbandry and market gardening to tailoring, cobbling, butchery, baking, and woodworking.

In 1938 the Welsh Valleys Subsistence Production Society recorded production of 242,590 pints of milk, 38,500 pounds of meat, 360 yards of blankets, and 69,499 concrete bricks.

Altogether around 900 people, mainly men, took part in the schemes in Wales and Lancashire. They remained on unemployment benefit and were not paid, but could take home the product of their labour and barter surplus goods among themselves, without suffering deductions in their dole money. Despite initial hostility from the local Labour party, trade unions and shopkeepers - some participants were stoned on their way to work - the schemes won many admirers, above all from the unemployed themselves.

PART FIVE:
COMMUNITY BUSINESS
IN AN AGE OF WELFARE

In 1942, in the midst of the Second World War, the Beveridge report was published. It caught the public imagination with an ambitious promise of a hopeful future and an end to the five 'Giant Evils' which Beveridge identified: squalor, ignorance, want, idleness, and disease.

The report formed the basis for the post-War welfare state, including the creation of the National Health Service. National Insurance was expanded into a comprehensive social security safety net for all citizens 'from the cradle to the grave'. This was accompanied by slum clearance, and improved education, maternity and children's services. At the same time a great part of the country's infrastructure was nationalised, including the Bank of England, the fuel, power and steel industries, and the railways. The aim was that these undertakings would be run for the benefit of all, rather than to the advantage of a wealthy shareholding minority.

It might have seemed that the need for community business had passed. Economic and social prosperity was now a matter for the State, working in a uniform way across the whole country, on an immense scale.

The achievements of the welfare state were indeed considerable. But by the 1970s it had become apparent that the Giant Evils described by Beveridge were still very much in evidence. Although the economy as a whole was growing rapidly, and while overall the standards of living improved substantially, the middle classes were gaining the greatest benefit and so economic inequalities and differences in life outcomes, far from diminishing, were actually increasing. In 1980 the Black Report revealed that the death rate for men in the lowest social class was twice that of men in the highest social class. Critics on both the left and right of politics claimed that the welfare state, despite all its achievements, was producing a damaging 'culture of dependency' and had failed to achieve Beveridge's intention that the state 'should not stifle incentive, opportunity, responsibility' but rather that 'in establishing a national minimum, it should leave room and encouragement for voluntary action by each individual to provide more than that minimum for himself and his family.' The welfare safety net was designed to stop people falling, but it needed to be accompanied by a ladder to help people raise themselves out of dependency.

And so, from the 1970s onwards, a new generation of community businesses emerged, especially in communities suffering most from unemployment, poor health, and ineffective public services.

Many of these community businesses started from the proposition that people themselves were a neglected resource. Too often treated as the 'problem', they were in fact the solution. The notion of 'asset based community development' took hold, particularly across a network of community development trusts dedicated to bottom-up regeneration. Development trusts sprung up across the country, running a variety of community business activities, with the declared intention of 'generating wealth in communities and keeping it there.'

The 1980s saw a rapid flowering of community business in Scotland, in response to soaring unemployment in urban areas and depopulation in remote rural communities, and this attracted worldwide attention, inspiring many in the development trusts movement in England.

As immigration increased in the 1970s and 1980s, new communities formed in towns and cities across England. Racial discrimination created barriers to jobs, housing and welfare services, but the creation of businesses set up and run by ethnic minority communities themselves were a sign of the determination and growing confidence of these communities.

During the 1990s and 2000s support networks were formed to make it easier to exchange experience and ideas, to provide practical assistance for start-up community businesses, and to lobby for greater recognition and investment. In effect, to build a movement. Over the last two decades the community business movement has steadily expanded in scale, moving beyond a few notable examples, to a great variety of successful and resilient businesses across the country.

Community-run pubs and shops have become an increasingly familiar feature of community life, especially in rural areas. Considerable advances have taken place in the acquisition of land for use by community business, above all in Scotland, where over half of the Western Isles are now in community ownership, restoring confidence and pride, and rekindling local economies.

Inspired by success in Scotland there has been considerable effort to increase community ownership in England. Many hundreds of community businesses have taken on redundant buildings from the public or private sectors, to provide a base for whatever services and facilities are most needed locally, as well as to generate independent income which can be applied for community benefit.

Place making:
there is another way

In the 1960's a decision was taken to build a raised motorway through the middle of the Ladbroke Grove and Portobello district of West London. In engineering terms, the new road was a triumph, the longest stretch of elevated motorway in Europe. But in community terms it was a disaster. Hundreds of homes had been demolished and as for the land left derelict under the motorway, the planners had given no thought to restoring it to local use.

But this was not a community which was likely to take things lying down. Back in 1958 the neighbourhood had suffered riots when racist gangs roamed the streets attacking West Indian families. The following year fascist leader Oswald Mosley stood for Parliament in the local constituency. The area had been afflicted by some of worst private landlords in the country, of whom Peter Rachman was the most notorious example. In all cases the response from community activists had been vigorous and determined. They had established the Notting Hill Carnival. They had set up a renowned housing association, the Notting Hill Housing Trust. They created the country's first neighbourhood law centre. Behind much of this was the Notting Hill Community Workshop which aimed to help local people 'wrest from the authorities whatever they decide their community requires'.

In 1966 the London Free School, based on an American model of self-organised learning, took over some of the derelict land which had been cleared for development of the motorway and used it for a temporary adventure playground. Subsequently the Playspace Group, led by local photographer Adam Ritchie, carried out an extensive community survey to find out what local people wanted, and drew up plans for a string of amenities, including shops, restaurants, play spaces and open spaces under the motorway. They lobbied the Greater London Council, the owners of the land, who had intended to use the derelict land for nothing more than car parking, and eventually their lobbying was successful: it was agreed that the land would be transferred into community ownership.

The North Kensington Amenity Trust, later renamed the Westway Development Trust, was set up in 1971, and it took over the 23 acres of blighted land under the motorway. In its early days, there was considerable conflict between left wing community activists and the Conservative-controlled local authority, both of whom wanted control over the new Trust. In the end it was decided that the Trust Board should consist of community representatives and council nominees in equal numbers, with an independent Chair.

The task however remained daunting: it now owned a desolate and dangerous 'twilight zone' of rubble and refuse. What should the Trust do, and who would pay for its work? At first the Trust achieved little, and depended entirely on council grants. But when Roger Matland took over as Trust Director in 1977 he brought a vision of community enterprise, inspired in part by Community Development Corporations in the United States.

Roger warned that it would take ten years to make the Trust self-sufficient. He was right, but by 1988 the Trust was independent of grant aid, and by the early 2000's it had created a string of community businesses in the spaces under the flyover: facilities for community groups, light industrial units, retail outlets, a fitness club, a skate park, and a sports centre which boasted the largest climbing wall in Europe.

The work of the Trust has attracted criticism at times. As a developer and landlord this was perhaps inevitable. It has had to balance its support for community activity with support for small businesses while at the same time managing a complex and difficult site. Rent levels have always been contentious, and at times the Trust has had to take a hard line with tenants who failed to pay their rent, no matter how valued they were by local people.

But nevertheless, the dereliction of the 1960s is now a distant memory. The strip of Trust land now provides one of North Kensington's main pedestrian thoroughfares. Three thousand shrubs and 500 trees have been planted and gardens and wildlife areas are dotted along the route. By 2016 the Westway Development Trust had become financially sustainable, with its sports and fitness activities alone generating over £4m income a year and receiving over 600,000 visits. Over 100 businesses, ranging from music promoters and designers to luxury lingerie and bike repairs had established their operations on the site. From its surpluses, and through partnership funding arrangements, the Trust is now capable of providing grants with a total value of £400,000 to 39 community projects, and providing 25 offices for local charities at one third of the prevailing market rent.

The example in North Kensington was soon followed by others. In the mid-1970s the South Bank area of London was a depressed and dying community, dominated by run-down buildings, empty warehouses, and derelict wasteland. In 1977 a developer announced plans to build on the site, but local residents were having none of it and were determined to put the community rather than private investors in the driving seat.

After a seven-year campaign Coin Street Community Builders

bought the site, borrowing £1m to do so. At Gabriel's Wharf a market with pop-up shops and restaurants became a neighbourhood attraction. With £2m raised from a merchant bank, after rejections by 30 other investors, the disused Oxo Tower wharf was converted into a mixed-use building with social housing run on a co-operative basis by the residents themselves, together with retail outlets and restaurants.

Coin Street Community Builders ran local parks and open spaces, and held annual festivals. They went on to build a nursery and later a Neighbourhood Centre, and also formed the South Bank Employers Group, an alliance of private companies and arts organisations committed to improve the neighbourhood. At a time when it was assumed by those in power that free-market capitalism was the only option, Coin Street Community Builders, just across the river from the Houses of Parliament, could claim 'there is another way.'

From early on the Westway Development Trust and Coin Street Community Builders attracted worldwide interest. In the UK, they played a leading role in the 1992 creation of the Development Trusts Association, initially a small band of 'bloody-minded' leaders of community businesses, none of whom seemed to understand the meaning of the phase 'it can't be done'.

Among the first members was Paddy Doherty, who had formed the Inner City Trust in Derry in Northern Ireland in 1981. Although Paddy was a prominent Republican civil rights activist, known as Paddy Bogside, the Trust was organised on a non-sectarian basis. Its first venture was a backpackers' hostel in the centre of Derry. Within a week of opening it was blown up by the IRA. Paddy gathered his supporters around the bombsite. 'Look at it now', he said to them, 'and think of all the trouble and hard work we put into it. But I'll tell you one thing, it will be a lot easier the next time round.' Not only did they rebuild the hostel, but many other projects followed: a crafts centre, a museum, a heritage centre, a multimedia and film centre, supported housing, and a luxury hotel. 'It's always better to seek forgiveness than to ask permission,' Paddy would say.

In 1994, 14 residents of the Thornton Estate in the heart of Hull decided to band together and tackle the social ills that plagued their community. They had decided that enough was enough, and they set up the Goodwin Development Trust, driven by a spirit of 'hard work, hope, help, goodwill, compassion and ambition.' Twenty years later they were employing a workforce of 200 people along with 140 volunteers. Their community business portfolio grew to include children's centres and nurseries, a state-of-the-art conference centre, a community college, disability care facilities, sports pitches, a youth and arts centre, performance space, and meeting rooms.

More recently they have expanded into affordable housing, refurbishing 60 empty homes and making them available for rent to local people, and also building five terraced houses on the estate using modular construction and with advanced environmentally sustainable features such as rainwater harvesting and grey water recycling. As the Trust Chief Executive Peter McGurn put it, 'We're a poor estate in a poor city. We try to look after people in the best way we can.'

In 2002 the Development Trusts Association published 'Fabulous Beasts', showcasing the development trust model across the country, with examples from Stocksbridge in Sheffield, Amble on the Northumberland coast, Carnarvon in North West Wales, Ferndale in the Rhondda Valley, Millfields in Plymouth, Burslem in Stoke on Trent, Knowle West in Bristol, Dingle in Liverpool, and others in Middlesbrough, Nottingham, Hull, Bradford, Barrow in Furness, and Hastings.

As it matured the network of development trusts could boast an almost endless procession of community businesses: local shops and pubs, restaurants, community farms, children's nurseries, craft centres, tourism, sports and fitness facilities, park and woodland management, local festivals, renewable energy, workspace and conference facilities, community housing, community transport, to name just a few. In all cases, surpluses were applied for additional community gain, by way of extra community services, and grants for local projects.

Much of creative energy which helped these community businesses to flourish came from the idea of 'asset based community development', the insight that it is better to start with the things which people and communities can do, rather than what they cannot, and build on strengths and aspirations rather than focus on weaknesses and obstacles. This generated a positive, hopeful, on-the-front-foot attitude, and the development trusts model spread across the country.

Development trusts became leading proponents of what were sometimes described as community 'anchors', In other words organisations capable of making sustained connections across the local community and voluntary sector, and also connecting those without voices with those in the public and private sectors who had power and influence, in order to build collaboration and common purpose.

Some development trusts won public sector contracts to deliver local services including job training schemes, community safety, and health promotion. This brought its own challenges: while it certainly increased the scope and scale of activities, increasingly the terms of the contracts ceded control to municipal authorities, creating predetermined and standardised forms of service delivery, and constricting the ability of the development trusts to work intelligently with their communities. Could they maintain their independence and creativity, or would they become 'an arm of the state', absorbing the very bureaucratic practices that they had railed against? It was, and continues to be, a difficult balancing act.

Nevertheless, the development trusts movement flourished. As Ed Mayo, then Director of the New Economics Foundation, said, 'this is not a politics of left or right, or a politics of self-interest or altruism. It is a politics of the imagination. It is the day you or a neighbour step over the broken pavement or the rubbish dumped in a doorway and say, not 'someone' should do something, but 'we' should do something.'

By 2010 there were almost 500 development trusts across the UK. In Scotland, Northern Ireland and Wales the networks of development trust continue to grow in numbers, confidence, and impact. In England in 2011 the Development Trusts Association merged with Bassac, the network of settlements and social action centres, to form Locality, which now describes itself as 'the national network of ambitious and enterprising community-led organisations, working together to help neighbourhoods thrive.'

Immigration and enterprise

From the earliest phases of community business immigrants played a part, although their deeds were rarely awarded more than a footnote in the history books. The history of immigration is a history of aspiration, but also of a continual struggle against prejudice and discrimination. One response to the multiple social and economic barriers faced by immigrants was to develop solidarity and mutual aid within their own communities, and in this way they created the conditions for many forms of community business to flourish.

There has been a Jewish community in England since the time of the Norman conquest, often persecuted with violence or excluded from mainstream trades and forced into economic occupations on the edge of society. The need for mutual help and support in an often hostile climate led to many Jewish communities setting up friendly societies, which played an important role in the lives of Jewish immigrants from the late 19th century and for much of the 20th century.

The earliest recorded Jewish friendly society was The Tent of Righteousness Friendly Society. A notice reporting their 1902 annual general meeting at the Elephant and Castle Hotel expressed their pride in being the oldest Jewish friendly society, founded in 1812. Another early example was the United Brethren Benefit Society, first mentioned in the Jewish Chronicle in 1847. This was a typical example of a Friendly Society or 'Chevra' created by working class Jewish immigrants. Members would club together to save a few pennies a week from their modest incomes to put into their societies, and benefit would be paid back in times of hardship such as bereavement, unemployment, and illness. Unlike many other friendly societies, they also ran religious activities, study circles and instruction of young people. By 1901, there were 176 in London alone. Beatrice Potter described the Chevra in London's East End as 'self-creating, self-supporting, and self-governing communities' although she also noted that they were culturally conservative and that women were strictly segregated.

In the early 19th century, among those advocating for community enterprise and ownership as an objective of social revolution, were several pioneering African-Caribbean radicals. One was Robert Wedderburn, the son of a Jamaican slave, a follower of Thomas Spence, and a member of the Society of Spencean Philanthropists. In around 1810 Wedderburn opened a Unitarian chapel in Hopkins Street, Soho and government spies reported that he was making 'violent, seditious, and bitterly anti-Christian Spencean speeches.' In 1817 Wedderburn wrote, 'The earth cannot be justly the private property of individuals, because it was never manufactured by man; therefore whoever sold it, sold that which was not his own.' By 1819 up to 200 people were paying six pence a head to attend debates and lectures 'every Sabbath day on Theology, Morality, Natural Philosophy and Politics by a self-taught West Indian.'

Frustrated in their attempts to promote Spence's Plan through rational argument, the Society turned to armed insurrection. In 1820 after the fiasco of the Cato Street conspiracy, its leaders, including another Black radical, William Davidson, were executed. Wedderburn himself opposed the conspiracy, but only because he thought it was premature. Eventually he was charged with blasphemous libel. In court he asked the jury: 'Where, after all, is my crime? It consists merely in having spoken in the same plain and homely language which Christ and his disciples uniformly used. There seems to be a conspiracy against the poor, to keep them in ignorance and superstition'. He was accused by the prosecution of being a 'dangerous man' with 'considerable talents'. Found guilty he was sentenced to two years in Dorchester Prison. On his release Wedderburn continued to campaign for press freedom, against injustice, and for the ideas of Thomas Spence. In 1824 he published *The Horrors of Slavery*. In 1831, at the age of 68, he was arrested once more and sent to Giltspur Street Prison; four years later he died.

Another remarkable Black radical who played a part in the story of community business was William Cuffay, born in Kent in 1788, the son of a naval cook and a former slave. By occupation he was a journeyman tailor, and in 1842 he became president of the London Chartists. He was an energetic supporter of O'Connor's Land Plan, and at the Chartists' 1845 national convention he proposed 'that the Conference now draw up a plan to enable the people to purchase land and place the surplus labourers who subscribe thereto on such land.'

In 1846 Cuffay was one of London's three delegates to the land conference, and together with another tailor, James Knight, he was appointed auditor to the National Land Company which soon had 600 branches all over the country. He received praise for the way in which he conducted this role: 'When hundreds of working men elected this man to audit the accounts of their benefit society, they did so in the full belief of his trustworthiness, and he never gave them reason to repent of their choice. Cuffay's sobriety and ever active spirit marked him for a very useful man; he cheerfully fulfilled the arduous duties devolved upon him.'

After the failure of the third Chartist petition Cuffay was accused of promoting an armed uprising, He was arrested, condemned to transportation, and died in poverty in Tasmania's workhouse in 1870.

Britain began trading with China in the 17th century and a small community of Chinese sailors grew up around Limehouse in East London, expanding over the next two centuries, with Chinese communities also taking root in Liverpool, Swansea, Cardiff and elsewhere.

Chinese benevolent associations, the earliest of which was the Chee Kung Tong, formed in Liverpool in the 1880s, played an important role in looking after the interests of their members, arranging burials, and assisting in cases of exploitation. In the early 20th century the Chinese communities faced growing hostility, with crowds of angry British seamen, opposed to the cheaper Chinese crews, preventing Chinese seamen from signing on ships. New benefit associations were formed, including the Hui Tong Association, set up in 1906 or 1907 in Poplar and Liverpool. Its stated aims were to organise mutual aid, improve Chinese living standards in Britain, fight discrimination, overcome disunity, and adjudicate in disputes between members, although allegedly it also engaged in criminal activity.

In 1916 the Zhong Shan Mutual Aid Workers Club was established in Liverpool, later moving to East London, and offering a meeting place free from British ridicule and humiliation. It aimed to unite the overseas Chinese in Britain, to improve their working conditions and to look after their welfare. Eventually the Zhong Shan Mutual Aid Workers Club moved to Soho in the West End, showing films and arranging classes, and organising the Chinese New Year celebrations in Gerrard Street.

By 1930 there were over thirty Chinese shops and restaurants in Limehouse, including several tobacconists and lodging houses. Chinese restaurants and cafés were the main social hub of the local community, providing a venue in which to conduct business, and serving secondary functions as informal post offices and banks.

Clan associations had been set up in the UK from the 1880s, with their roots in a particular family lineage or district of China, but from 1963 when there was large scale immigration from Hong Kong, these took on a bigger role. The Cheung Clansmen Charity Association dominated the Chinese restaurant sector, leading the way in the colonisation of Gerrard Street, and others including the Man and Pang clan associations also accumulated property and business interests.

Between 1955 and 1962 over 480,000 Commonwealth citizens came to live in Britain. Tighter immigration controls were then imposed, with an average of 75,000 immigrants per year in the 1960s and 72,000 per year in the 1970s, particularly from the West Indies, India, Pakistan and Bangladesh, as well as Asian refugees from East Africa in the 1960s and 1970s.

At first, housing conditions were grim, as immigrants had to live in Britain for three years before being allowed to join a waiting list for local authority housing. During this time, as indeed in the decades to follow, immigrants were often forced to endure slum conditions in badly maintained private rented accommodation owned by rogue landlords. From 1955, however, housing associations were set up to help immigrants. The first were in Leeds, followed by Birmingham, Nottingham and London.

In the late 1980s, following riots in Brixton, Toxteth and elsewhere, some 40 housing associations led by people from Black and ethnic minority communities were established with funding support from government, with the aim of providing affordable housing for African-Caribbean, Vietnamese, Chinese and Asian populations, and thereby addressing social inequality.

Some of these associations grew rapidly. In 1979 The Asra Project (meaning shelter in Hindi and Urdu) grew out of Family First in Nottinghamshire, in response to incidences of elderly Asians becoming homeless, living in isolated conditions and suffering from physical and verbal harassment. With the assistance of Leicester Housing Association, the project later became Asra Midlands Housing Association, and in 1984 a sister association was set up in London. Asra grew from under 100 homes at the end of the 1980s to nearly 2,000 a decade later and now has 14,000 homes.

Steve Douglas, who ran Asra in the 1980s, and who later became Chief Executive of the Housing Corporation, looked back on those years: 'There was a real energy there – there were people who had been disadvantaged, who were young and bright and were dissatisfied with the status quo and who had ideas actually articulating those, having them listened to and being given some level of authority.'

But growth brought its own problems. The increasing scale of public and private investment into the housing association movement came at a price. Across the whole housing association sector, public bodies imposed an increased burden of regulation and restrictive design specifications, and the associations lost control of housing referrals, making it impossible to establish balanced communities, and yet more 'sink' estates were produced.

At the same time, the requirement for private as well as public investment, and growing professionalisation of the sector, led to acquisitions and mergers, and the creation of a powerful group of very large housing associations, which had little if any community identity or allegiance. Indeed, some became aggressive and predatory businesses, in effect stripping wealth from one community in order to finance expansion into the next, and although there were sporadic attempts to stimulate a 'housing plus' agenda, in order to encourage social and economic development activities for residents and for the wider community, these were at best a side-line as far as large developers were concerned, who became ever more seduced by the potential to build housing for sale in the private market, and ran their operations as increasingly commercialised businesses.

The effect of this was to marginalise and undermine many community-led housing associations. Some were forced into mergers, and others closed because of lack of investment or internal mismanagement. Black and ethnic minority-led housing associations were hit especially hard: the doors to public investment started to close, and failures and frauds in a few were given the highest possible profile, tainting by implication the entire movement. Many were absorbed into group structures which subsequently wound them down, assimilating their housing and removing their unique identity.

Yet a few managed to thrive, either within their new groups, like Ashram which has become Ashram Moseley within the Accord Group, or independently. In total around 70 Black and ethnic minority-led independent housing organisations have survived. While most are small, managing less than 1,000 homes, they provided 65,000 homes in total in 2016, with an estimated annual turnover of £600m and controlling assets valued at around £1.8bn. It is estimated that they invest some £150m yearly in their local communities, through local procurement, as well as neighbourhood facilities, skills and employment projects, well-being activities, community safety, and environmental schemes.

Over the years successive generations of immigrant communities have brought with them their own models of mutual aid. For example, lending circles are found around the world, wherever poor people exist, systems of state welfare are inadequate, and access to formal banking is out of reach. Examples include the 'stokvel' model in South Africa, where groups of twelve or more people contribute periodically to a shared fund, and in each period the total contributions are disbursed to one of the members, by rotation. Operating on trust, and with no-one making profit or charging interest, this has become highly popular and it is estimated that there are now 800,000 stokvels in existence, with one in every two Black adults in South Africa in membership. In the UK, similar schemes have been brought over by successive waves of migrants. They operate under many different names, 'pardner' within Caribbbean communities, 'ayuuto' or 'hagbad' in Somali communities, 'sou sou' in other East African communities, 'committee' in Indian communities, and so on. These help to maintain the culture and practice of mutual aid, and in some cases become the platform for wider social initiative, for example when the members of the lending circle decide to set aside one of the periodic 'hands' or withdrawals for a charitable purpose.

Within immigrant communities, the distinction between private and social business has often been blurred. Trade and enterprise has always been a means to grow both private and community prosperity, to build a better life for a widening network of family, friends and neighbours. Enterprises established by such communities were typically characterised by a combination of self-help and self-organisation, mutual support within existing communities and for new arrivals, and activities intended to challenge or ameliorate discrimination. In some cases the enterprises were also a vehicle for building a community of faith. Much of this remains the case today.

In 2002 ex-banker Eric Samuel began buying produce from Spitalfields food market, loading it into his van and taking it to local estates. Community Food Enterprise now operates across some of the poorest neighbourhoods in East London, with breakfast clubs at schools, lunch clubs for the over-50s and juice bars at local events, and a mobile food store which travels to the estates. It also runs cook-and-eat sessions, with courses offering nutrition, cookery and business skills.

In 1990 Jawaahir Daahir, a lecturer and radio broadcaster fled civil unrest in Mogadishu in Somalia and moved to Holland. Ten years later, she brought her children to Leicester, and established Somali Development Services to support the Somali community in the city and Somali women in particular. It provides drop-in advice sessions and help with education, employment, health, housing and family support. There is also a homework club, English and IT classes and a youth outreach programme.

PJ's Community Services was established in 1992 as a family-run business headed by husband and wife team Patrick and Claudine Reid, which now employs 20 staff and offers services to Black, Asian and Minority Ethnic communities, with a focus on fitness, faith, family, and finance. It operates from a multi-purpose centre in Croydon, South London with music recording studios, a children's day nursery, office space and meeting rooms, and also offers home care, a health and social care recruitment agency, and business development support. In 2008 Claudine Reid was voted as one of Britain's Top 100 'Most Entrepreneurial Women' by Real Business Magazine.

The Selby Trust in Tottenham was set up in 1992, supported by local MP Bernie Grant, who had a vision for a place in the community that people could afford and call their own. It took over a redundant school on a lease from the local council, creating a multi-purpose community and social enterprise centre, with offices rented out to small businesses and charities, alongside meeting rooms, training facilities, and sports and events halls. Almost 80% of Selby Trust funding is now self-generated. It is located in an area of considerable deprivation, and brings together a rich mix of individuals and organisations, primarily from Black, ethnic minority, refugee and other historically excluded communities in Tottenham and beyond, and is run by people from these communities. As its Chief Executive Sona Mahtani said, 'We transformed a 1960s shell into a thriving hub that shows what a poor community can do for volunteering, self-help, jobs and social enterprise,' and the motto of the Selby Trust is 'many cultures, one community'.

In 2017 research by Britain Thinks for Power to Change revealed that the appetite for involvement in community businesses among people from ethnic minority communities was higher (20%) than among the White population (12%). A reflection perhaps of the long tradition of mutual aid, enterprise, and community building among immigrant communities in this country.

A voyage significant and hazardous

The Craigmillar estate in Edinburgh was a suburb afflicted by high rise buildings and mass unemployment. In 1974 the Craigmillar Festival Society, which had organised an annual arts festival for over ten years, set up a working party to consider what could be done about unemployment in the area. This led to a series of Manpower Services Commission programmes, with over 150 people involved on various schemes. The experience and confidence gained led to an attempt to provide permanent, economically viable jobs and Craigmillar Festival Enterprises came into being in 1978. The primary goal of providing work meant a labour intensive operation, matching the skills of unemployed people. This led to the choice of a building and maintenance business run by local people and employing up to 20 local men.

However, the building industry was notorious for its rapid downturn and frequent business collapses, and the problem was exacerbated because the new company was unable to attract council contracts to work in the immediate neighbourhood. The need to operate further afield reduced the visible impact within the Craigmillar estate, and led to pressure to recruit employees from outside the estate to raise quality and compete in the private market. In 1981

Craigmillar Festival Enterprises closed with debts of £77,000. Board member Councillor David Brown put on a brave face, claiming that the major factor for the failure was the economic recession; 'Like other building firms we have suffered and we have gone to the wall' 'On reflection, he said, 'the decision to go into the building field was right, because we had the skilled people. No one could have foreseen the economic problems.'

In November 1977 the Highlands and Islands Development Board launched a Community Co-operative scheme, offering 'working capital' funding to be matched pound for pound by local people, alongside advice and support from field officers. The community of Ness on the Isle of Lewis was the first to respond, building on previous activities in the mid-1970s funded by an independent trust the Van Leer Foundation, which had included a horticultural project providing seedlings for crofters, and a small combine harvester used as a threshing mill.

In 1978 Co-Chomunn Nis (Ness Community Co-operative) was set up. 540 people (a quarter of the entire local population) contributed £20 each. The main trading activities were a horticultural project, sale of feedstuffs and fertilisers, veterinary products and protective clothing, a fish and chip van (later superseded by a mobile grocery van), a delivery service, and construction of new homes under contract with the local council. At its peak 15 people were employed in the various activities.

But there were problems, not least opposition from existing traders. Inadequate storage facilities, poor continuity of managers, inadequacy of record keeping and accounting, and lack of experience in costing the construction work, compounded the difficulties. The Highlands and Islands Development Board insisted that the Committee, made up of local residents, should not interfere with day to day management, but on the other hand managers brought in from outside lacked local knowledge and it was observed at the time that 'the experience of running other businesses was rarely an adequate training for the business of running community co-operatives.' There was little opportunity at that time to network with other community co-operatives, and so it was not possible to learn from the mistakes and successes of others. After a series of losses came to light, the co-operative went into liquidation in 1986.

Both Craigmillar Festival Enterprises and Co-Chomunn Nis had made mistakes, but along the way they inspired others, and so proved to be the start of a first modern-day flowering of community business across Scotland in the decade from 1980 to 1990.

Once famed for shipbuilding around the world, by the 1970s Govan on the edge of Glasgow was in decline. For those living there, the town's motto 'Nihil Sine Labore' had assumed a new meaning: 'Nae sign o' work.' As John Pearce, a leading community business activist at the time was later to explain: 'The old housing stock was demolished and, with it, the small shops and commercial premises which had helped the local economy to survive. Govan became a blackspot for unemployment and, with a lack of suitable premises, was unattractive to new businesses or to established businesses wishing to relocate. Poverty and disadvantage was rife and the morale of the community at an all-time low.'

Govan Workspace was set up in 1981 by local people to tackle these problems by creating Scotland's first community workspace. Like many community businesses, it was a defiant and positive local response to the economic and social challenges of the time, which many in Scotland regarded as the consequences, at least in part, of a policy determined by a far-away government in London.

The workspace idea was, at the time, novel, but like most good business ideas it was also simple: bringing redundant buildings into community use, providing space from which local businesses could operate, together with administrative and copying/printing facilities, or other forms of support. In that way, it was hoped, something could be done to rekindle the local economy, and also if possible generate a surplus from the rental income which could be applied for community benefit.

By 1987, Govan Workspace had a turnover of £350,000, and 85 tenant businesses were occupying units and employing over 400 people. The manager Pat Cassidy was able to state 'We're at the stage now where we are confident that the company will survive.' But he also emphasised the need for perseverance. 'Nothing is going to happen overnight, particularly in terms of raising finance.' he said. 'The timescales are enormous. Since 1981, when I started working as manager of Govan Workspace, I've always seen ten years as the timescale for development.'

Now, 35 years since he started, the company has indeed survived and Pat Cassidy is still there. Govan Workspace has gone on to acquire further buildings and now has assets of £4.6m. In 1996 Alexander Stephen House, a former shipyard headquarters, was brought into community ownership and now provides 23 high-quality offices. In 2009 the Fairfield Shipyard Offices which had been lying empty and derelict since 2001 were purchased; the building now provides office space alongside a resource centre telling the story of Govan's shipbuilding heritage.

Not all community businesses were run by and dominated by men. At Possil Community Business women were the driving force. In 1984 a steering group was formed in Possilpark, an inner-city housing estate in Glasgow, which faced 40% unemployment and high levels of drug abuse. The steering group comprised local residents, social workers, and housing department officials and sought answers to two questions: 'How much investment was there in Possil?' and 'What skills existed in the area which could be used inside or outside the area to create jobs?' What emerged were three community businesses: a cleaning company, a neighbourhood security company, and a painting/decorating squad.

The cleaning company was called Kleencare and was set up by five local women. They had identified a market opportunity: a large number of new-build private and housing association properties on the borders of their estate requiring cleaning services. Community Business Scotland designed a package of support to help them: courses in industrial and domestic cleaning at Glasgow College of Food Technology, courses in business administration, and a capital grant for equipment and working capital. They started trading in 1985 and described themselves as the 'Glasgow female equivalent of Auf Wiedersehen, Pet!'

By 1986 there were 59 community businesses in urban Scotland and 21 community cooperatives in the Highlands and Islands, and the number grew to over 100 by the end of the decade. Their range of activities was very wide, and indicated considerable community ingenuity and flair. They included community shops, hotels, peat cutting, knitwear, crafts, salmon farming, furniture upholstery, a coal merchant business, fishermen's supplies, community transport, tractor hire, an art gallery, a restaurant, a pub, a laundrette, holiday accommodation, and property services, often running a workspace.

Most of these community businesses ran multiple ventures. Forgewood Enterprises in Motherwell ran a daytime café which doubled as a night-time carry-out fish and chip shop, as well as hire of hillwalking boots and cagoules. Brag Community Enterprises in a coalfields district of Fife ran workspace in a converted primary school, and later set up a community transport scheme to help people in outlying villages get to work, partly funded by local employers. Ferguslie Park Community Holdings in Paisley ran a hairdressing business as well an enterprise which carried out tenement rehabilitation and graffiti removal for local councils. On the Islands, Eday Community Enterprises began by building a small supermarket and followed it with a commercial peat-cutting venture and a youth hostel converted from a redundant community hall.

What made community business special? According to Susan McGinlay from Possil Community Business, it was, at heart, an ability to see 'what people could do, not what they couldn't. To look at people and not be judgemental or negative, but to be positive about them. That is what the community business is about, investing in people.'

Enthusiasm was high, but it was not always accompanied by business success. Support agencies, notably the Highlands and Islands Development Board, Strathclyde Community Business, and Community Business Scotland attempted to foster business skills through consultancy and training, and through peer-to-peer networks. They were demonstrating that, from small beginnings, it was possible to build a nationwide movement. But for many it was a bumpy road. As Tony Worthington, Chair of Community Business Strathclyde, said in 1986, the voyage of community businesses was 'at once more significant and more hazardous' than its advocates had at first realised.

There were some who were looking for an opportunity to condemn the whole movement. Scepticism that residents in poor neighbourhoods could ever make a success of business was accompanied in some quarters by downright hostility, as municipal socialists on the one hand, and free-market conservatives on the other, came to regard this small but vigorous and high-profile network as nothing less than a threat to the established way of doing things.

Their opportunity came in 1990 with the collapse of Barrowfield Community Business. The visibility of this particular community business was exceptionally high, and it had probably received more international visitors than any other in Scotland. Since 1984 it had achieved a great deal. It had pioneered neighbourhood security as a community business, and its landscaping and environmental business had transformed the appearance of the area and 'demonstrated that if local people do local work it is more likely to be valued and to last.' A local authority tenement block had been converted into offices and light industrial workspace, and at its peak Barrowfield Community Business had employed around 100 people in its commercial enterprises and over 150 in its Community Programme and training projects, most of whom had been long-term unemployed.

So why did it fail? Already in 1986 and 1987 Strathclyde Community Business had noted slackness in bookkeeping and financial irregularities, and had urged consolidation rather than further expansion. But these warnings were not acted upon. By 1988 income from a European Social Fund grant and private sector contracts was used to support general cash flow, national insurance debts were building up, and the pricing of new contracts was being done on an uneconomic basis. As John Pearce from Community Business Strathclyde explained, there were other weaknesses as well: 'There were continuing management problems; it proved virtually impossible to find the 'right' person to manage the complex organisation. The enterprise overstretched itself - often encouraged by public and private sector agencies equally caught up in the exciting momentum of action - in terms of the number of projects and businesses it became involved in.'

The insolvency practitioner who investigated recommended that £100,000 be injected into the community business to keep it going because of the social value of its work. However, the local councils decided they could only judge the matter on business support criteria. On these criteria alone the business was deemed to have failed. New investment was refused and the organisation, including all its subsidiaries, was forced into liquidation.

Two reports by respected academic Keith Hayton were published in 1993 and 1996. 'The picture that emerges,' said Hayton, 'is of a number of businesses involved in marginal activities that can be entered because the capital requirements are small and some preferential terms can be obtained from those who award public-sector contracts. The sectors they occupy, such as security, are equally open to conventional small firms and are therefore very competitive.'

Hayton was especially critical of the business viability of many community businesses, claiming that they seemed to be 'mainly interested in meeting the needs of their local communities and employees, especially as regards creating jobs, rather than the needs of their customers. Their objectives are therefore heavily biased towards a social rather than an economic emphasis which must undermine their long-term goal of becoming self-sustaining.' Only one third were judged to be making a trading surplus.

He did however note that some had been successful, were trading viably, and were able to create new jobs at an average cost of £4,450, which compared well with other job creation programmes. In his view, the most successful community businesses were those where the priority for managers was 'commercial success rather than any wider community benefits.' 'Community management' seemed to Hayton a 'recipe for disaster' involving 'little emphasis upon long-term strategy and a very reactive short-term approach to decision making.' A much better approach, he suggested, would be the 'involvement of the wider community as customers,' as this would require that the business provided a service that residents wanted and were able to use.

No doubt some of this analysis reflected broader attitudes in the 1990s, which saw a shift in favour of managerial and market-driven models of public service. But nevertheless, the closure of Barrowfield Community Business and the subsequent Hayton reports had repercussions throughout the world of community business and brought into sharp focus key questions about which criteria should be used to judge success and failure. The situation was not helped by local government reorganisation in Scotland in 1994 which led to the sweeping away of regional councils. At a stroke, the community business movement lost many of its remaining public sector allies, and funding for the support and development agencies almost disappeared, or was channelled into new directions.

The vulnerability of the community business movement was compounded by chronic undercapitalisation. With very few exceptions these community businesses suffered from a lack of unrestricted reserves, the absence of an asset base in the form of ownership of land or buildings, and few opportunities to access investment capital. A weak balance sheet not only restricted the prospect of expansion and growth, but also meant that when times were hard there was no buffer and therefore a negative cash position was always just around the corner. It was an important lesson, and one which was very much taken to heart by the next generation of community businesses.

Because, inevitably, there was a next generation. For a while the term 'community business' was tainted in Scotland and fell out of fashion with policymakers and funders. Yet many organisations did survive, changing their names to avoid the stigma, rebranding themselves as 'community enterprises' or 'development trusts' or 'social enterprises'.

Possil Community Business, for example, evolved into the Allander Group, and its security and cleaning businesses are still trading. As Susan McGinlay, founder of Kleencare and now a Board member of the Allander Group said, 'Not everything was successful, but here we are 30 odd years on still going strong.' Looking back, there was much to be proud of: 'You think my God all the work that we have created in this area. It rejuvenated quite a lot of the people, it really did. It was a turning point for very many of them, who started to see what they could do and what they were worth, rather than being told oh you come from Possil or Milton and you are scum and you are this and you are that.'

And this core idea, that community business offers a way of investing in people, in order to help them improve their lives and their community, never disappeared. It was taken forward by the development trusts movement in England and Wales and Northern Ireland, and in Scotland it was to resurface in spectacular fashion a decade later, as the 'community right to buy' movement gathered pace in the Highlands and Islands, and a development trusts network, initiated by Laurence Demarco and Aidan Pia from Senscot, created a second flowering of community business across Scotland which continues to the present day.

All right then, why don't you buy it yourselves?

The Red Lion is an attractive Victorian pub in the small Hertfordshire village of Preston, accessible only by narrow winding country lanes, four miles from Hitchin, the closest market town.

When the pub manager died in 1980, the owners Whitbread thought they had a golden opportunity to make money, by turning the Red Lion into a large, steakhouse-style restaurant, all the fashion at the time. However, there was one thing they had not allowed for: the reaction of local residents. A protest meeting held at the village hall was attended by most of them and they made their views abundantly clear. They just wanted, they said, a 'simple place' where the cricket team, the darts team, the Hunt and the Morris dancers could meet and 'make merry'.

The villagers launched a vigorous campaign to oppose the development, lobbying the local councillors to withhold planning permission and arranging for the building to be listed. In the event, to the great relief of the villagers, and perhaps also to their surprise, the planning committee rejected Whitbread's application. Whitbread immediately announced their intention to appeal. The villagers responded by raising funds to continue their campaign.

One Sunday, the villagers 'sacrificed a pig to save a Lion': to raise campaign funds they had a hog roast on the village green, attended by around 200 people.

Seeing the determination of the villagers, Whitbread abandoned its plans for the steakhouse. Instead, they decided to sell the pub. The residents made it clear that they would resist any changes, no matter who bought the place. So, according to Richard Beharrell, one of the campaigners, the brewery said, 'All right then, why don't you buy it yourselves?'

The asking price was £125,000 and a further £10K was needed for initial operating expenses. Given there were just 130 households in the village, this must have seemed a tall order. Nevertheless a company limited by shares was formed, and households from within a distance of three miles were invited to buy shares, with a minimum subscription of £1. In the event, the share issue was successful. By the end of 1982, an astonishing £95,000 had been raised, and a bank loan of £40,000 covered the shortfall. The Red Lion now belonged to the people of Preston.

But extensive renovations were needed, as Whitbread had allowed the building to fall into serious disrepair. 'We had problems with the roof and the insulation – we had to change the staircase, the kitchen would not have met the health requirements, and we had to create living quarters for the manager,' said Beharell.

The villagers rallied round, drawing on their collective resources, which fortunately included an expert in restoring old buildings. 'Everyone who was able to lend a skill – carpentry, decorating, expert advice or moral support – was mobilised. Older folk, who were unable to help, donated plants and trees.'Volunteers remarked that they had 'hung enough wall paper to cover the village green.'

The Red Lion re-opened on 19 March 1983. Today it is full of character, immaculately maintained, and has won the CAMRA North Herts pub of the year award four times since 2000 as well as the national Good Pub Guide's 'Value Pub of the Year 2014'. And it is still owned by its community: at July 2015 a total of 168 local residents owned £92,392 shares, in amounts ranging from £1 to over £20,000.

Other community pubs followed, notably Tafarn y Fic, a pub in Llithfaen, near Pwllheli in North West Wales, which was bought by local residents in 1988. It thrives to this day, and is especially celebrated for its Welsh language musical evenings. In this case a community co-operative structure was used, to ensure that it would remain forever in social ownership, and that has formed the model for most community pubs subsequently.

In recent years there has been a steady rise in the number of community pubs, in part due to the efforts of the Plunkett Foundation, Locality, and CAMRA. The Plunkett Foundation estimated that by July 2016, fourty-two communities had successfully taken ownership of their local pub, and a further 1,250 had been listed as 'assets of community value' under the 2010 legislation.

Often community groups have chosen to locate multiple services in pubs, making them the hubs of their local areas in more ways than one. For example, the Old Crown is an 18th century pub in the village of Hesket Newmarket, on the northern edge of the Lake District National Park. When the former owners of the pub retired, the villagers feared that the pub might fall into the hands of a major brewery and that its unique character would be lost. 125 customers of the pub clubbed together to buy it, each contributing an equal shareholding of £1,500, and assisted by grant funding: the Old Crown reopened as a co-operative in 2003. The commitment and enthusiasm of the group was a catalyst for the pub's development, and resulted in a new dining and meeting room, and a broadband ICT facility with links to the local primary school which won 'Best Outreach' at the UK online centres awards in 2008.

Another community pub that offers more than a pint is the Anglers Rest in Bamford, Derbyshire, which was purchased in 2013 by over 300 people from the local area. This building not only houses the pub itself, but also a community meeting venue, a café, and a local Post Office.

And some have been remarkably successful. In March 2017 the George and Dragon at Hudswell in North Yorkshire hit the national headlines when it won the national CAMRA Pub of the Year award. It was praised for its welcoming atmosphere and strong community ethos, its range of real ales and ciders, and its beer terrace, which offers panoramic views over the Swale Valley. The George and Dragon hosts the village library, a local shop, and community allotments. As Stu Miller, the pub landlord said: 'We're a small Yorkshire Dales pub, owned by the community and run by me and my family, I'm extremely proud of what our little pub has achieved.'

It is one thing establishing a community pub in a relatively prosperous rural setting, where there is a fair chance that there will be an abundance of people with professional skills and deep pockets, but what about in a depressed council estate?

On the Moulsecoomb and Bevendean estates on the outskirts of Brighton, there were no bank managers and retired insurance brokers. 'We've got retired bus drivers and community workers and midwives and hospital workers. We don't know the buttons to press so much and we don't have the financial clout,' said local resident Warren Carter. The Bevendean Hotel, better known as The Bevy, was the only pub serving a population of 18,000. Its reputation was not good. In 2006 an on-line pub review warned potential customers 'not to upset the locals from the tough surrounding estates unless you enjoy a 10 on 1 fight'. It was closed by police after a series of violent incidents in 2010 and put up for sale, but there were no buyers.

So a group of local residents decided to take it on. They persuaded a local housing association, the East Brighton Trust, to buy the site, convert the upper floors for housing, and provide them with a long lease to operate the pub. But in the meantime the pub's fixtures and fittings had been stripped out, and £200,000 was needed for refurbishment. Shares were sold to 660 people, with a minimum subscription of £10, raising £70,000, and a further £130,000 was provided by a social lender, the Social Investment Business. To keep costs down, local people helped to fit out the space. The Bevy reopened on 12 December 2014.

'I'll be honest, it's been hard work,' said Warren Carter, who took on the role of chair of the Bevy community pub committee, 'especially with its past reputation and the fact that pubs have changed. It needed to be more than a pub. We are more of a day centre than just a pub. We have lots of things going on here; a running club, seniors club and also quizzes and bands – but we still have the traditional feel.'

Further growth of the community pubs movement is expected. March 2016 saw the launch of the More than a Pub initiative, a £3.6m programme, jointly funded by the Department for Communities and Local Government and Power to Change. Its aim is to support another 80 community owned pubs which can 'demonstrate how they will bring significant social, economic and environmental benefits to their communities'.

This is all happening at a time when the benefits of a good local community pub are receiving academic recognition. In January 2016 CAMRA published research by Professor Robin Dunbar from Oxford University which revealed that 'people who patronise community-type pubs have more close friends on whom they can call for support, and are happier and more trusting of others than those who do not have a local. They also feel more engaged with their wider community.' Heavy drinking was significantly less common among those regularly using community-type pubs, compared to casual pub visitors and those using large chain pubs. And as Professor Dunbar said: 'Given the increasing tendency for our social life to be online rather than face-to-face, having relaxed accessible venues where people can meet old friends and make new ones becomes ever more necessary.'

We've become trendy

Local co-operative stores had proliferated in the second half of the 19th century, and in 1863 300 individual societies in Yorkshire and Lancashire established the North of England Co-operative Wholesale Industrial and Provident Society Limited to benefit from bulk-buying opportunities. By 1872 this was known as the Co-operative Wholesale Society (CWS) and was wholly owned by the co-operatives which traded with it.

The CWS grew rapidly, and established factories for the manufacture of biscuits in Manchester, boots in Leicester, soap in Durham, and textiles in Batley. In an attempt to drive down the cost of transportation the CWS even began its own shipping line which sailed from Goole docks to continental Europe. The CWS went on the establish the CWS Bank, the precursor to The Co-operative Bank, financing loans to societies to use for purchasing new buildings, land, or equipment. From 1913 the CWS acquired the Co-operative Insurance Society, and also began providing legal services.

However, tensions were always present between the fiercely independent local societies and the national CWS. As far as many local societies were concerned, the powerful CWS became the tail that wagged the dog, especially when the CWS attempted to establish itself as the monopoly provider of goods and services to the co-operative movement, and to centralise and professionalise the whole operation. And certainly, after the Second World War, the CWS marketed its products to the upwardly mobile sections of the population rather than the traditional working poor, and local community identity came to be seen as a liability rather than an asset.

The CWS nevertheless continued to innovate, establishing a market leadership position in self-service stores, expanding its banking operations into the personal banking market, and pioneering free banking nine years before any of its larger rivals. Many of the local societies merged, to form regional groups, but these did not always prosper, in part because they were burdened with complex and ineffective leadership and management structures.

All the modernising measures seemed to be of no avail during the 1970s and 1980s when the co-operative retail movement went into a steep decline, as deindustrialisation reduced spending power across its traditional customer base, and market share was lost to aggressive commercial competition, better positioned to appeal to an increasingly consumerist society. By the 1980s, it became clear that the trend in the retail sector was towards large out of town supermarkets and hypermarkets with hundreds of them appearing across the UK, and the co-operative movement seemed destined to become a thing of the past.

Eventually the fragmented and quarrelsome co-operative operations were brought together into a single national Co-operative Group. Despite catastrophic mismanagement of The Co-operative Bank in recent years, the retail operations have revived under a renewed brand and stronger leadership and today the Co-op stores retain a significant presence across the country. But while the customer dividend has been reintroduced, and some attempts have been made to increase local purchasing, to provide grants and other support to local charities, and to present the Co-op as an ethical retail option, the Co-op stores are no longer community-led businesses.

However, the decline and disappearance of the traditional community-based co-operative societies did not spell the end for the community shop. In rural areas, a new generation of community owned and run shops appeared in the 1990s. The impetus for this was the widespread loss of local family-run village shops, with around 200 closing every year due to commercial pressures from big supermarkets, as well as post office cuts and rising rental costs.

A village shop in Itteringham in Norfolk had been trading since 1637 as a family run business, but in 1994, following the death of the owner, it seemed it would be lost forever. So local people decided to have a go at running it themselves. It worked and has been run as a community shop ever since. It now has an annual turnover of £100,000 and about 25 people out of the 120 who live in the village help run the store. According to volunteer Mike Hemsley: 'We celebrate Norfolk food now and were doing that back in 1994. The curious thing is we've become trendy.'

There are now 337 community shops across the UK. Peter Couchman from the Plunkett Foundation, which played a major role alongside the Esmee Fairbairn Foundation in helping community shops across the country get off the ground, said 'We think we've reached a tipping point where we have now gone from a few communities doing something that others saw as unusual to a situation where people are now thinking they could do it too. It is seen as a credible, viable option. It is incredibly rare for the shops to fail, closure rates are virtually zero.'

In 2009 a community shop was opened in Almondsbury, a village on the outskirts of Bristol. Volunteers from the village run the shop which provide a wide range of goods with an emphasis on fresh, local produce, minimising the miles travelled. In 2010 it became the inspiration for the fictional community shop in long-running radio drama *The Archers*, which brought the story of community shops to a wider audience.

In Barford in Warwickshire, it seemed that the shop-cum-Post Office would be consigned to the village's history when the previous owners retired. With a Sainsbury's and Lidl just four miles away in Warwick, selling four pints of milk for £1, how could a village shop possibly compete? But a group of villagers decided to set up a community interest company, with shares owned by 530 villagers, in order to establish a local shop, run by a team of 80 volunteers, with all profits going back to the community, and with a mission to support local producers. And it has been able to generate significant surpluses. Since it opened in 2008, £86,000 has been handed over to help fund a new village sports ground, to pay for street lighting, computers and a piano for the local school, and even a flagpole for the village green.

Dunsfold Community Shop in Surrey was created when the previous owners announced their retirement after 28 years, and no commercial buyers could be found for what was the last shop in the village. The shop had served the village for over 100 years and a survey of local people found that 95% said it was very important to them. The community buy-out was launched in 2011 and attracted 220 local investors, who between them invested £208,130. The shop now also incorporates a post office and a dry cleaning service, and serves teas and coffees. As one local customer says: 'The shop has everything you might need, I am a regular visitor and the service is always warm and friendly, it is a pleasure to shop somewhere where I am always greeted by name.'

Community shops depend heavily on local customer loyalty, and some make great efforts to reach those who are isolated or housebound. The Broadwindsor Community Shop in Dorset offers a free delivery service while Ashton Hayes Community Shop in Cheshire started an assisted shopping service for villagers who would otherwise find it difficult to shop on their own.

New models are emerging all the time, and not only in rural settings. In 2010 the People's Supermarket opened in Holborn in London, with the aim of providing good cheap food to its local community. Inspired in part by the Park Slope Food Co-op in Brooklyn in the

United States, it operates a membership system, whereby members pay a £25 annual fee and contribute four hours of their time every four weeks to working in the store. In return, they receive a 20% discount when they shop at the People's Supermarket.

In 2013 hiSbe, which stands for 'how it should be', opened in Brighton, with a full range of food and groceries. It avoids big brands, sources locally as much as possible, and refuses to throw away food that can be eaten. It runs as a community business, and aims to 'put happiness before profits'.

Also in 2013, a pilot 'social supermarket' opened in Goldthorpe, near Barnsley. Its membership was open only to people on welfare benefits, and the aim was to provide low cost food while at the same time helping people into work. This model relies on a relationship with commercial supermarkets, which donate food (but not tobacco or alcohol) nearing its sell-by date or which has been rejected because of damaged packaging or incorrect labelling. At the same time personal development programmes, designed to 'kick-start positive change' in the lives of the members, are provided for up to six months. The pilot in Goldthorpe was successful, with 500 people joining as members, and subsequently a branch was set up in South Norwood in London and another in Athersley in Yorkshire, this time in partnership with the Coalfields Regeneration Trust.

Today, we live in a period when patterns of retail consumption are changing fast, with a trend away from out-of-town supermarkets, heightened awareness of the need to reduce food waste, and above all a rapid expansion of internet grocery shopping. Will the movement of community shops be able to rise to the challenge of these changes and expand still further? If the adaptability and inventiveness of the past is anything to go by, the answer may well be yes.

To have
and to hold

Back in 1917 William Hesketh Lever, the industrial philanthropist and founder of Port Sunlight, had bought the island of Lewis and two years later the neighbouring island of Harris. Lever then embarked upon a bold plan to transform the economy of the islands by modernising the fishing industry. There would be an ice-making factory at Stornoway, refrigerated cargo ships, and a canning factory. To create a market for the islanders' fish, Lever bought up 350 fishmongers' shops throughout Britain, creating the Macfisheries chain. The venture became known as 'Port Fishlight'.

But the grand plan was never fully realised. Lever's high-handed attitude towards the crofting way of life created local animosity, and in 1923 he abandoned his plans, offering instead to transfer all the land by way of gift to the crofters and to district trusts. The islanders, deeply mistrustful, turned down the offer. Only Stornoway council accepted the gift, setting up the Stornoway Trust and taking possession of 70,000 acres. For many years the Trust struggled to develop income streams, but in 1973 it leased land to a Norwegian oil company. This deal generated environmental concerns but produced revenues which made the Trust viable, and it is still running today.

It wasn't until 1992 that the spirit of community ownership was revived in rural Scotland. In that year the North Lochinver Estate, covering 21,300 acres and running from Achmelvich to Loch Nedd, was put up for sale in several small lots. For people living there, the prospect of a multiplicity of disinterested or negligent landlords loomed large. At a public meeting, the crofters resolved to mount a campaign to buy the land and secure the future for themselves and future generations. The Assynt Crofters' Trust was formed and took title to the land on 1st February 1993. In the words of the local MP, this 'lit a beacon throughout Scotland'.

Others followed. The Isle of Eigg had suffered particularly badly from absentee landlords, including a Yorkshire businessman who had hung a Nazi banner from Eigg Lodge, his island holiday home, and an eccentric German artist who preferred to be known as 'Maruma' a name which came to him while gazing into a pool of water in Abu Dhabi. In 1997 the islanders bought the island, providing at long last security of tenure for the crofters, and embarking on a series of community ventures: a restaurant and community centre, a community-run construction company, and an electrification scheme, combining water, wind and solar power, and reaching every household and business on the island.

In 2002 on the island of Gigha the residents raised £4m, and bought their island. The founding chairman of the Heritage Trust, Willie McSporran, had been a farmworker, fisherman, estate handyman and ferryman. As he said at the time of the purchase, 'this is only the beginning of a longer road'. The Trust managed to repay a £1m loan within two years, and now runs a quarry, a hotel, self-catering cottages, and business premises. It also runs Britain's first community-owned windfarm connected to the national grid: its three wind turbines are known as the 'dancing ladies', and the success of this venture has inspired by other community energy schemes across Scotland and elsewhere in the UK.

The movement of community land ownership, as a foundation for community business and community revival, spread across rural Scotland. Highlands and Islands Enterprise, the Big Lottery Fund in Scotland, Community Land Scotland, and the Development Trusts Association Scotland, all played a big role. New legislation, the Land Reform (Scotland) Act 2003, created a 'community right to buy' where the community could demonstrate a valid interest and popular support. It applied to both public and private land.

Half a million acres of land are now in community ownership in rural Scotland, equivalent to the whole of West Yorkshire. Community land ownership has brought new life to the Islands, the Highlands, and other rural districts in Scotland. And many in England looked on and thought, if it can happen there, why not here?

The Development Trusts Association, later Locality, redoubled its efforts to build the case for community asset ownership in England, as a foundation for effective and sustainable community business. It found influential allies. Charles Woodd at the Department for Communities and Local Government was instrumental in helping the Development Trusts Association establish an Asset Transfer Unit, designed to encourage local councils and other public bodies to review their property portfolios and transfer property into community hands, provided of course that sufficient benefits could be demonstrated. He also helped to get a 'meanwhile assets' initiative off the ground, to help community businesses take a temporary lease in empty property. There were allies within local government as well, and for example Tony Rich at the Local Government Association helped to open doors to community asset transfer in local authorities across the country. And in the private sector, Andrew Robinson at National Westminster Bank was among the first to recognise the potential for community ownership to stimulate business growth in broken markets, and together with Ed Mayo from Co-operatives UK, helped to set up the Social Investment Task Force.

But in all these cases, and in many others, it seemed that efforts to build momentum for community ownership were over-dependent on a small number of committed individuals, fighting against the grain of the institutions in which they operated.

Scepticism was widespread. Community ownership, it was said, would create liabilities not assets, diverting the energy, time and resources of community organisations into managing a building instead of delivering services, saddling them with the costs of running the building, and burdening them with the responsibility for repairs and dilapidations. Many in the public sector argued that community asset transfer meant 'selling the family silver' to a motley collection of unelected and unaccountable community activists. It was feared that community ownership would produce community division: in cases when organisations were competing for a building any decision to favour one over the other would produce an enduring legacy of community bitterness. Above all, it was claimed, community organisations, especially in deprived neighbourhoods, simply would not have the capability to manage things themselves. Everyone it seemed had a story to tell of community incompetence, of mismanagement, and even of fraud.

And yet, while there were setbacks, momentum continued to build for community ownership in England. A General Disposal Consent was introduced by Government which allowed a range of public bodies to transfer the ownership and management of land and buildings to local communities at 'less than best consideration', in other words at less than full market value. The Development Trusts Association published a detailed manual for community ownership by Lorraine Hart: To Have and to Hold, and accompanied it with other resources designed to reduce risks of community ownership, including an 'Early Warning Guide' to help Boards and managers of community businesses assess whether they were in good shape or heading for the rocks. The Asset Transfer Unit assembled legal and other professional skills, set up an advice line accompanied by consultancy support, ran seminars, and produced case studies as well as a series of specialist guidance notes, including a legal tool-kit.

And, best of all, there were more and more positive stories to tell. The Asset Transfer Unit estimated that between 2007 and 2012 there were around 1,500 asset transfer initiatives across England. The Development Trusts Association's 2010 survey found that within the previous 12 months a great variety of land and buildings had been taken over for community purposes: disused industrial buildings, redundant offices, empty restaurants, boarded-up shops, residential housing, old school buildings, closed libraries, wasteland, parks and recreational space, youth hostels, enterprise parks, former chapels and churches, woodland, and pubs.

Alongside these developments, there was mounting public and political concern about the shortage of affordable housing in both rural and urban areas, especially in the South of England, but increasingly in other parts of the country as well. This led to a great deal of interest in the idea of a 'community land trust', a model which had originated in the 1960s Civil Rights movement in the United States, designed to overcome discrimination in the allocation of public housing and the availability of private mortgages, and produce long-term opportunities for economic and residential independence for African Americans in the rural south.

Over the last two decades the community land trust idea has been vigorously promoted in England as a solution to the crisis of affordable housing. By means of a community land trust, it was argued, a community could acquire land, through a gift of the land, or by raising finance, and develop it for housing and other purposes, sometimes with the involvement of commercial developers. The important thing was that the community would always retain ownership and control of the land itself. By doing so, the uplift in land value which would result from development of housing and any other facilities could be captured for community benefit rather than for private gain, and this would mean that housing affordability could be 'hard-wired' into any new housing development.

This idea was not new in England: a century earlier the original garden cities had used the same model, and more recently several development trusts, notably Coin Street Community Builders, had been highly successful in developing affordable housing by applying equivalent principles. But nevertheless the concept of a community land trust proved to be an effective and attractive brand, and from 2006 to 2008, a national demonstration programme was funded by Carnegie UK Trust and Tudor Trust, and in 2010 a National Community Land Trust Network was established to support the growing movement and advocate on its behalf.

Many community land trusts have taken shape in rural areas, and most operate on a small scale, and yet they can nevertheless have a transformative impact on their community. Off the coast of Northumberland is the island of Lindisfarne, renowned for the monastery founded by St Aiden in 635AD and the Lindisfarne Gospels produced there half a century later. Over the succeeding centuries this tiny island community suffered a succession of calamities, including Viking raids, the dissolution of its monastery, and land enclosures, but somehow always recovered. But by the late 1990s the future was looking bleak. While there was no shortage of tourists eager to experience the beauty of this iconic place, a lack of affordable housing was threatening the viability of the community of people who lived on the island: the younger generation simply could no longer afford to live there. The population was falling and in 1998 the local school was mothballed for lack of pupils.

Today the island is home to a community of around 180 people. Local people have set up a Community Development Trust which runs the tourist centre and maintains the inner harbour. The Trust has renovated the coastguard lookout tower and created a 'Gospel Garden'. Most importantly it has found ways to build affordable homes, initially using charitable funds and subsequently government grants from the Homes and Communities Agency, and it was the first community organisation which was not a registered housing association to do so. Ownership remains with the trust, rents are not linked to land values, and the homes cannot be sold under right to acquire rules, so affordable homes will continue to be available for the benefit of future generations on the island. Now a fifth of the permanent islanders and half of the schoolchildren live in homes provided by the trust, and the school has reopened. The future of this ancient community now looks much brighter.

PART SIX:
COMMUNITY BUSINESS
IN AN AGE OF AUSTERITY

Austerity is nothing new, and as we have seen community businesses have been a response to economic hardship, unemployment, social dislocation, and the erosion of local facilities and services over many centuries.

And yet the economic crash of 2008, the most severe global downturn since the Great Depression, marked a new chapter in the story of community business in England. A consequence of the financial crash was the decision by successive governments to impose mounting reductions in public spending, and the poorest sections of the community were worst affected. This was accompanied by a loss of confidence in public institutions and in economic globalisation, as well as mounting concerns over climate change.

All of this has had profound implications for community business. On the one hand, failures of both private and public sector models and of centralised 'top-down' solutions have reinforced the arguments in favour of localised self-determination and more social forms of enterprise, possibly even pointing the way towards a new post-globalisation era.

On the other hand, the immediate operating environment has become more difficult, with growing tension and estrangement at neighbourhood level, and mounting demand for welfare assistance. Withdrawal of public sector subsidy for community business operating in areas of market failure has been exacerbated by a 'race to the bottom' in public sector pricing, with a tendency for commissioners to seek economies of scale through standardisation and transfer of activity to large private sector corporates.

Enabling legislation was introduced in 2011 to provide

mechanisms for community business to express interest in and acquire 'assets of community value', and to make a case to run local services. And while the community business sector remains undercapitalised, there have been fresh attempts to provide new investment, including the setting up of Power to Change with a £150m endowment from the Big Lottery Fund. Most notably, the use of community shares, first seen in the 18th century, has been revived with great success.

So far, community businesses have on the whole proved more resilient than many other parts of the social sector to the pressures of austerity. At a time when neither the welfare state nor the free market can be relied on to produce universal prosperity and social well-being, and with the instinct for community self-organisation and self-determination as strong as it always has been, the community business movement continues to grow.

Community rights

By the turn of the millennium, community business across the UK was gathering pace as a movement. The conventional assumption that a successful community business could only be the product of a very unusual set of local circumstances, and required a truly exceptional leader, seemed increasingly doubtful. Community businesses were flourishing in every type of locality, and while good leadership was certainly important, it seemed that it could be found in any community, including the very poorest. Even government started to take notice.

From 2003 onwards pressure was building for an English version of the Scottish 'community right to buy' and for a fresh look at the relationship between the town hall and its local community. Barry Quirk, Chief Executive of Lewisham Council, accepted a government invitation to lead an Inquiry into community ownership.

His report was launched in 2007 at the Burton Street Foundation in Sheffield, where the local council had transferred a redundant school into community ownership. Here, the asset transfer had created the conditions for a thriving community business, which had seized the opportunity of a new 'personal budget' funding regime to expand its work with people with disability, and at the same time had raised finance to refurbish the building, with space for 50 local businesses and community groups, as well as a gym, recording studio, restaurant, training facilities and a bar. As the Foundation could claim, 'It's a pretty special place'. The question was, could asset transfer lead to something equivalent in other places across the country?

'Imagine this' were the opening words of the Quirk Review. 'It is 2020 and communities across England have been revitalised from within'. The report's endorsement of the principles of community ownership became highly influential, encouraging a fresh wave of community asset transfer. It also reinforced the demand for a better framework of enabling legislation in England.

Locality led the charge, building an evidence base and a network of influential champions, including the Local Government Association, the Charity Commission, and the Big Lottery Fund, accompanied by independent funders, think tanks and academics, and winning allies across the political spectrum and within the civil service.

This work culminated in the 2011 Localism Act, which introduced a community right to bid, a new legal framework designed to encourage transfer of assets to community ownership. The community right to bid provided an opportunity to apply for land and buildings of community value to be listed by the local council. It also created a six month window if the property came up for sale, giving the community a chance to raise funds and submit an offer.

This provision applied to both private and public buildings, and encountered fierce opposition from the Country Land and Business Association, an organisation which had recently changed its name from the Country Landowners Association in an attempt to improve its public image. It was particularly concerned that the community right to bid could disrupt property inheritance among the 35,000 people (less than half of one tenth of one per cent of the population) who own half the land in England and Wales. But nevertheless Conservative Minister Greg Clarke stood firm and with cross-party support the Act was passed.

By February 2015, 1,800 assets of community value had been successfully listed. In some cases, the local authority embarked on multiple community asset transfers. For example, in Kirklees in 2014, the council embarked on an Asset Advancement strategy. With support from Locality, eight community asset transfers had been completed by the end of 2016 and a further seven were in the final stages of completion. One was the Meltham Carlile Institute, an empty building on the town's high street, which had long been in a poor start of repair. Three residents were determined to transform it into a versatile, sustainable hub for their community. They established a Community Interest Company in February 2014 and applied for the building to be listed as an Asset of Community Value. Asset transfer was completed in September 2014. Then followed a refurbishment of the ground floor of the building using funds from Kirklees Council and others, enabling the post office to move into the building and the office space to be leased out to businesses, generating an income of £32,000 per year. The community business is now run by 20 local people, and attracts 6,500 users a year. In 2016 Meltham Carlile CIC was awarded a further grant from Power to Change to complete the refurbishment of the building, improve disability access and expand its operations, with plans to provide offices for the Town Council and host the local library.

Alongside the community right to bid to promote asset transfer, the Localism Act also introduced a suite of other powers which together became known as 'community rights'. These included a community right to challenge which allowed local organisations to submit an expression of interest in running a local council service. If the expression of interest was accepted, the council would then be required to run a tender process or some other form of procurement for the service. In practice this power was rarely used, as to do so could strike an adversarial note in the relationship between a local community and the local authority. But its very existence prompted the question in neighbourhoods across the county: could any of the local services be better delivered by a community business?

The Localism Act also introduced powers for communities to draw up a neighbourhood plan, creating a framework for people to identify community priorities and give them legal force in the planning system, provided that the plan could pass an independent inspection and gain local support through a community referendum. And alongside neighbourhood planning, the Localism Act introduced yet another mechanism, a community right to build. This allowed a community to draw up a Community Right to Build Order, which, if supported in a local referendum, would enable a small scale local development to go ahead without going through the normal planning application process.

Exeter St James was the first urban community to complete the neighbourhood planning process in February 2013. A local community consultation discovered that the few allotment plots that were in existence on the railway embankment were highly valued by the community and that residents were keen to increase the number of plots. The neighbourhood plan included a provision that proposed development would not be allowed if it resulted in harm or loss of allotments, and stated an intention to work on improving the use of the existing allotments. Since the plan came into force, the railway embankment allotments were revamped and renamed the St James Vegetable Gardens. Sunday morning working parties worked on maintenance tasks, clearing shared spaces and potential vacant plots, and completing a new eco-friendly rainwater collection system.

None of these powers by themselves were game-changers. But, at the very least, they provided official sanction for the idea that some land and buildings and some local services could be better run by local people as community businesses. With central government funding, Locality, Plunkett Foundation, Co-ops UK, the Social Investment Business, Community Matters, the Community Development Foundation and others ran a series of national programmes designed to raise awareness and provide practical assistance to communities to take up the new community rights. This included 'Our Place', a nationwide programme which encouraged public, private, and community bodies to come together in a neighbourhood, pool their budgets, and work with local citizens to identify priorities, in an effort to provide a better co-ordinated set of local services. A national programme was also launched to recruit and train community organisers, with the aim of 'igniting the impulse to act' within local neighbourhoods, where objectives were set not by government or even by local agencies, but by local people themselves.

The Localism Act and the accompanying local programmes were regarded by the Coalition Government of the day as part of its Big Society project, which was launched in 2010 and which aimed to give communities more power and to encourage philanthropy and volunteering, while at the same time reducing the role of 'Big Government'. The Big Society project was criticised for many reasons, not least for a 'year zero' approach which alienated many of its natural supporters in the voluntary and community sector, and its importance as an instrument of public policy declined from 2013. A majority of the population were suspicious about the Big Society project from the start, regarding it as a 'cover for cuts', an indication of how difficult it is for any government to promote a community-led model of social change while reducing public sector spending.

Indeed, it seemed that many of the gains for community during this period were made despite rather than because of the Big Society project. Libraries were a case in point. Across the country, faced by the need to reduce public spending, local authorities closed hundreds of libraries. There was widespread public anger but those leading the Government's Big Society project seemed unsympathetic. In communities where libraries were closing people demonstrated against the council or central government, calling for cuts decisions to be reversed. But others decided to take on the local library themselves, and turn it into a community-run venture.

In rural areas community-run libraries soon appeared. In 2011 in Farnham Common in Buckinghamshire the library was transferred to the community on a 25 year lease on a peppercorn rent. The community library now benefits from over 50 volunteers. It receives a grant from the council as well as support from the council's library service, and generates its own income from a Friends Group membership fees and rent from a children's centre and the local police service. Against national trends, the number of users has increased.

In urban settings too, communities took action. After a long and high profile campaign which attracted international attention residents in Kensal Rise in North West London saved their local library, which had been opened by Mark Twain in 1900, and which was under threat of closure by a cash-strapped local council. Using the Localism Act powers to list the library as an asset of community value, the community eventually negotiated a long lease on part of the historic building. As Margaret Bailey, Chair of the library Friends group, said in 2016, 'it will be more than a space with books and computers. We plan to run classes and workshops and activities and projects that meet the needs and interests of all in the community. We want to make the library a force for good.'

It wasn't all plain sailing. Some people had concerns about the sustainability of community libraries. Community groups had to try to demonstrate that after the initial flush of enthusiasm they would not decline and fade away. There were also challenges to overcome to developing more entrepreneurial models, most significantly a deeply embedded culture which made it very difficult to reconcile the desire to provide free access to all users with an entrepreneurial mind-set.

However, it became clear that there were opportunities, not least because of the prime location enjoyed by many libraries. The Upper Norwood Library Trust with support from Locality, the Libraries Taskforce, and the Society of Chief Librarians, established a national network of community-run libraries to help them exchange ideas. Some community libraries demonstrated imaginative potential for income generation, for example through alignment with other public sector services, creating 'hackspaces' or 'makerspaces', deals with on-line traders to establish pick-up points for deliveries, sales of advertising, running cafes or leisure businesses and the sale of books or other articles.

By 2017 the Community Libraries Peer Network had 202 members. Over half had benefitted from community asset transfer. In many cases community management had led to a revived service, with longer opening hours and more users. Most retained a relationship with the local council, whether in the form of access to library stock, support from professional librarians, or grant aid. It seemed that the survival of community libraries would depend in large measure on the continuing quality of community-public partnerships, as well as the ingenuity and commitment of local people.

The community rights and the wider localism programmes were not designed specifically to nurture community businesses. But they were intended to stimulate community-led action, and to promote community confidence and self-determination. And so, despite their limitations, they helped to create the conditions for the community business movement to gather strength and legitimacy, even in the harsh climate generated by austerity and public spending cuts.

Investing
for good

Community businesses in the past had always sought the funding they needed to get off the ground from every possible source, but until recently the options had been very limited.

As we have seen, in the 18th and 19th centuries friendly societies and other mutual aid associations had raised finance for community businesses from their own members and a wider community of supporters, and in the 1840's Feargus O'Connor had raised £100,000 through selling shares in his Land Plan, about £25m in today's terms. Robert Owen had hoped that government could be persuaded to finance his 'villages of co-operation', but that never happened. Owen spent his own fortune in establishing co-operative ventures, and hoped that other wealthy philanthropists would follow his example, but, then as now, there were never enough wealthy philanthropists to do more than point the way.

Independent grant making trusts have long played their part in supporting community businesses, notably the Nuffield Trust and Carnegie UK Trust in the 1930s and the Calouste Gulbenkian Foundation in the 1980s. Subsequently others, including the Northern Rock Foundation and the Lankelly Chase Foundation, demonstrated that small amounts of grant funding could go a long way in the hands of community entrepreneurs. One notable grant funding success in recent years was the Esmee Fairbairn Foundation's £1.7m community shops programme, delivered by the Plunkett Foundation and assisted by Co-operative and Community Finance. Between 2006 and 2012, combining grants, small loans, and expert support, it helped establish 90 new community shops across the UK.

In the mid-19th century, as we have seen, O'Connor's Land Plan had been closed down by the government when it was declared an illegal lottery. Today lottery money is a significant source of finance for community business. In Scotland over the last decade Big Lottery Fund grant programmes have played a major role in boosting community asset transfer and community enterprise, and similar programmes were set up by the Big Lottery Fund in Wales. In England the Big Lottery Fund had long supported community businesses through its main grants programmes, but realised that more could be done. In January 2015 it established the Power to Change Trust, a new grant-maker dedicated to community business, with £150m to spend over a ten year period.

While commercial bank finance was out of reach for many community businesses, especially those at the earlier start-up stages, a series of social lenders emerged in order to provide loans to the growing community business and social enterprise movement. An early example was the Local Investment Fund, set up in 1995 with funds from government and National Westminster Bank, which provided loans ranging from £15,000 to £75,000. Its founding director, Andrew Robinson, went on to become head of community development at NatWest/RBS bank, playing a prominent role in the development of an investment market for community business. Unity Bank, Triodos Bank and Charity Bank all built up a portfolio of lending to community businesses, and a network of community development finance intermediaries was formed, with some like the Aston Reinvestment Trust in Birmingham operating locally, and others like CAF Venturesome operating on a national scale. Unlike commercial banks, social lenders were sometimes able to offer unsecured loans, and operate at a higher level of risk. In 2002, Government introduced community investment tax relief to stimulate the flow of private finance via intermediary social lenders for community businesses operating in deprived areas across the country.

But it became clear that loan finance by itself was not sufficient. A 'blended finance' model was pioneered by the Key Fund, offering packages of grants and loans accompanied by practical support. The Key Fund was established in Sheffield in 1999 to counteract the scourge of long-term unemployment after the collapse of the steel and coal industries, and now operates right across the North of England. It claims that its 'northern soul' has 'national clout', and with good reason: its model of blended finance, built on trusted relationships between investor and community business, has been widely admired.

In 2002, the Adventure Capital Fund was launched as an England-wide investment vehicle for community businesses, drawing on the Key Fund experience. It was a partnership of the Development Trusts Association, the Local Investment Fund, the Scarman Trust, and the New Economics Foundation. With funds from central government, it was able to provide a package of feasibility grants, business advisors, and blended grant/loan investments, tailored in each case to the specific circumstances of the community business. The Adventure Capital Fund went on to create the Social Investment Business and to deliver a £70m government-funded 'Community builders' programme, helping community businesses across England acquire land and buildings and build up their business operations. Following the Localism Act in 2010 further government funding for community assets and community-run services was made available via the Social Investment Business, supporting over 750 community businesses with grants ranging from £3,000 to almost £500,000.

A social investment wholesaler, Big Society Capital, was set up in 2011 with £600m, principally from dormant bank accounts.

Community business leaders, notably Iain Tuckett from Coin Street Community Builders, had long lobbied for a social investor capable of combining public and private finance for community business. But Big Society Capital was designed to grow a market which could attract further private investment, and consequently its finance was largely limited to large scale enterprises which were able to offer security and afford relatively high interest payments, with loan deals typically in excess of £150,000.

In order to widen the benefits of social investment to smaller organisations including community businesses, the Access Foundation was launched in 2015. Its aim was to apply grant funding from government and the Big Lottery Fund to rebalance the work of Big Society Capital, making it possible for social lenders to offer blended packages of smaller scale loans, alongside grants and capacity building support, drawing on the experience of the Key Fund and Adventure Capital Fund.

An important recent milestone was the 2012 creation, again with central government backing, of the Community Shares Unit by Co-ops UK and Locality following a five-year collaboration. Here at long last was national encouragement and support for community businesses to help them build a base of local people with a direct stake in a community venture. Community shares quickly became a major success story. Since 2009, almost 120,000 people have invested over £100m to support 350 community businesses throughout the UK through community shares. Pubs, shops, renewable energy schemes, food and farming businesses, sports and community facilities were all raising community finance in this way.

One high profile example was Hastings pier. Opened in 1872, the pier had quickly become a much loved feature of the town, boasting a pavilion for concerts and plays, and a landing stage for excursions along the South Coast and even trips across the Channel to Boulogne. In the 1930s it was given an Art Deco revamp and in August 1931, 56,000 people passed through the turnstiles. In the 1960s and 1970s it played host to a succession of famous names including The Rolling Stones, The Who, The Kinks, Jimi Hendrix, Pink Floyd, The Hollies, The Clash and The Sex Pistols. But in the 1980s, like so many other piers, it fell into disrepair and was eventually closed in 2008. Two years later, in October 2010, it was virtually destroyed by a fire. But the community refused to give up, and following a compulsory purchase order by Hastings Borough Council, Hastings Pier Charity bought the pier for £1 in August 2013, with the ambition of restoring it and reopening it to the public. A development plan was put forward to the Heritage Lottery Fund, which awarded a grant of £11.4m towards the £14.2m needed for restoration. Additional grants were raised to meet the remaining funding gap, but it was a community share scheme which has attracted over 4,700 shareholders and raised close to £850,000 which finally secured the future of the pier as a community business.

At Dingwall near Inverness, plans are well advanced to create Scotland's first community-run whisky distillery. The loss of the former Ferintosh distillery in the area, which dated back to the 17th century, had been long ago lamented by the poet Robert Burns, who wrote: 'Thee, Ferintosh! O sadly lost! / Scotland lament frae coast to coast!' But Scotland need lament no longer. In 2016, 270 years to the day after the battle of Culloden, GlenWyvis Distillery Community Benefit Society issued a community share issue. Within 77 days it had raised £2.5m from 2,456 investors.

The success of any social movement depends in large part on its ability to tell a convincing story about the difference it can make. But describing the impact of community businesses has proved to be surprisingly difficult. While individual stories have always been powerful and influential, in recent years there have been repeated calls for a more robust 'evidence-based' way of assessing impact. This was felt to be important for two reasons. Firstly, to help community businesses 'improve' by understanding their impact and identifying what they could do better. Secondly, to help community businesses 'prove' the value of their work, and therefore convince others including policy makers and investors.

Back in the 1980s considerable effort was put into this by Community Business Scotland, which pioneered a Social Audit approach. It had become clear at the time that if the success of community businesses was to be measured simply in conventional business terms, such as the levels of trading profitability and the financial return on investment, many would be seen as failures. A method was needed which could also audit community benefits. This led to work by John Pearce and others to design a system of social accounting, by which community benefits could be described, measured, and independently verified by trained social auditors. A social audit check list produced in the mid-1980s set out seven objectives for any community business, all of which could be measured through a social audit: to create jobs for local people; to provide local services; to be good employers; to set up a community owned and controlled enterprise; to benefit the community; to use profits for community benefit; to act as a focus for local economic and community development.

A social audit network was established to promote the practice across the growing world of community business. Social audit proved a useful tool for talking about social purpose with multiple stakeholders and assessing whether progress was being made. It may well have helped some community businesses rethink their operations and improve their social outcomes. However, it was probably less successful in convincing others of the credibility of community businesses or in attracting investment. The attempt to use social audit for these purposes was also not helped by questionable practice in the private sector, where it was appropriated by international corporations, including oil and mining giants, as part of a corporate social responsibility strategy that many saw as superficial.

In 2002 the New Economics Foundation introduced a new impact measurement tool: LM3. This was a response to a phenomenon described as the 'leaky bucket': top-down regeneration programmes were pouring large sums of government money into deprived areas but somehow these places seemed to remain as poor as ever. Why was that? The New Economics Foundation pointed out that the vast majority of the regeneration spending was on consultants and contractors from outside, so as fast as the money was pouring in it was leaking out. The challenge was to capture inward investment in neighbourhoods and keep it circulating locally, and the LM3 tool helped to measure the local multiplier effects when spending was redirected through local supply chains, for example when local people were employed, and spending locally. Community businesses seized the opportunity to use the LM3 tool themselves. Hill Holt Wood, an award-winning community business which provides life-changing training in a woodland setting for young people excluded from school, was able to demonstrate a LM3 score of 2.43. In other words every £1.00 of investment from Lincolnshire Country Council into the services provided by Hill Holt Wood produced £2.43 of circulated spending in the local area, capturing wealth in the community and keeping it there.

For a while the focus of attention shifted to Social Return on Investment (SROI), a methodology pioneered by the Roberts Foundation in the United States. This was an attempt to identify the monetary value of social outcomes, and compare the investment (the cost of a delivering a social project) with the social return (the amount saved). For example Liverpool-based community business Bulky Bob's, which diverts bulky waste from landfill, identified various ways in which it was achieving social return: 'through increasing local and national taxation revenues and reducing benefits payments when unemployed trainees find sustainable employment; by reducing expenditure on landfill; by giving low-income shoppers the opportunity to buy great quality pre-loved furniture and to avoid using expensive credit; and by generating revenue from waste sources'. By giving this monetary value, a social return on investment ratio could be established: in this case £2.50 for every £1 invested. Initially the SROI approach was eagerly championed by Government, which regarded it as a means to attract greater private investment into the social sector. But many remained unconvinced. SROI methodologies were expensive to administer, and it seemed to its critics that the ratios of return on investment were all too easily capable of manipulation.

An underlying difficulty in any attempt to describe the social impact of a community business is the problem of attribution. Most community businesses carry out a variety of different activities, with complex interactions between them, and individual beneficiaries may gain a great deal or very little from these activities, and therefore standardised SROI projections are rarely helpful.

Moreover, if the community business did not exist, some things would improve 'by themselves', and this needs to be taken into account. In most cases any beneficial outcomes are the result of a combination of multiple interventions, by many different agencies, not simply by a single community business. Because of all of this, the true cause and effect or 'attribution' is very difficult to determine in an honest way, and in a way that convinces others. Randomised control trials and long-term longitudinal studies are, in theory, able to overcome these difficulties, but in practice, they are far too difficult and expensive to implement as far as the overwhelming majority of community businesses are concerned.

In the end, it seems that most attempts to describe the impact of community businesses still depended upon storytelling, preferably by the broadest possible spectrum of people with lived experience of their community, and if possible through a 'collective impact' approach which combines evidence across local agencies and sectors. The search for a 'holy grail', an impact methodology which is straightforward and low cost to apply, and which can gain universal acceptance, will no doubt continue.

In the meantime, most community businesses continue to take a pragmatic approach. They routinely generate evidence from some form of monitoring process. Sometimes they commission external evaluation so that what they assert can be independently verified. And if they want to understand their impacts more deeply, they organise discussion groups with members of their community. In some cases community businesses have recruited and trained local people to act as community researchers, often then selling a community research service to others, in true entrepreneurial spirit.

Against all
the odds

Over the last decade, as year by year the public spending cuts bit deeper, community organisations in every part of the country have found it increasingly hard to keep their heads above water. Some have gone under.

For many of those that have survived, the impositions of a public sector contracting regime have had a pernicious effect. An 'economy of scale' mentality has produced ever larger contracts and many smaller-scale community business have been forced into sub-contracting roles, in which their ability to shape services for the benefit of their communities has been all but lost. A focus on unit costs has created a race to the bottom in pricing, giving the appearance of saving money to the public purse, but missing the point about how value is created at community level, and storing up problems for the future. 'Payment by results' mechanisms have become all the fashion, promising a focus on social change and flexibility of action, but in practice forcing community businesses into transactional behaviours designed to satisfy narrow policy objectives set by funding bodies. While it is certainly the case that some community businesses have expanded the operations by winning public sector contracts, as a general rule, the contracts have reduced the scope of community businesses for independent action, disincentivised collaboration, and forced services into pre-determined patterns, making it much harder to deliver what community organisations do best, that is, building relationships, responding flexibly to the endless complexities of lived experience, and designing services with a human touch.

And yet, during this difficult period, the community business movement has more than held its own, and in many cases has continued to flourish and to grow. While the movement is by no means immune from the effects of spending cuts or the contracting culture, nevertheless its ability to generate independent income through trading and its entrepreneurial can-do spirit have served it well.

For example in 2016 Locality reported that its 600 members in England owned £779m of assets, with £372m income, including £261m earned income, primarily from public sector contracts and other trading activities. And other sections of the community business movement have reported strong progress. According to the National Community Land Trust Network there are now over 170 community land trusts and similar forms of community led housing, in both rural and urban areas, across England and Wales. More widely, Social Finance estimated in a 2016 report for Power to Change that there were over 7,000 community businesses of all types in England. This included 1,300 'community hubs', 1,100 sports and leisure community businesses, and 1,000 community transport schemes. The report also claimed there were 900 community businesses engaged in food catering and production, 520 in craft industry and production, 340 in environment and conservation, 340 in energy, 315 in housing, 75 in health and social care, and 75 engaged in digital activities. It also estimated that the community business sector included 330 community shops and cafes, 300 community libraries, 300 community arts centres, 150 credit unions, and 40 community pubs.

These figures do not provide the whole picture, as many community businesses engage in multiple activities. Nevertheless they do indicate the scale and breadth of the sector. The Power to Change report suggested that between them community businesses controlled £2.1 billion of assets, and achieved over £1 billion of income.

Behind every one of these statistics are stories of community determination, creativity, and enterprise. To take just three examples:

In 2006 Saffron Lane Neighbourhood Council in Leicester took over took over 12 acres of disused allotments, creating Saffron Acres. This led to a jam making business, with jam and chutney made by students with learning difficulties from Leicester College. The business was successful, recently winning an order for 6,000 jars from the regional Co-op supermarket chain. More recently this small community business has built the biggest development of eco-friendly affordable homes in the country on an adjoining 13 acre plot which for years had sat empty, derelict and filled with weeds.

The open-air swimming pool at Portishead was always rather special, with panoramic views over the Bristol channel. But in 2008 it was threatened with closure by North Somerset Council. The community rallied round, and within a year the swimming pool was transferred on a 99 year lease to a Community Trust, which carried out a major refurbishment, including a new restaurant and a biomass boiler to produce green energy for the pool.

In 2009 The Lynemouth Community Trust formed a chocolate and fudge making business, called Kenspeckle Northumbrian Confectionary. Kenspeckle is a Northumbrian dialect word meaning 'distinctive', and that is certainly true of its products. One of the most popular is 'edible coal', a cinder toffee centre covered in edible black dust chocolate, inspired by Lynemouth's coalmining past, and now sold at Selfridges in London's West End.

The significance of this national growth of community business is especially great in a local context. Many local authorities are coming to realise that a network of local community businesses, capable of working in partnership with public and private sectors, and harnessing the ever-present ingenuity and determination of local citizens, offer at least a partial solution to the challenges they face.

'I've got no room left for manoeuvre,' Liverpool Mayor Joe Anderson said in 2017. 'I've cut the fat, then the flesh. Now I'm down to the bone.' And yet today there is a flourishing community business movement in Liverpool, and while this cannot fully compensate for the loss of core public services, it can at least contribute to a collective effort to maintain the city's prosperity and pride, and ensure that its most vulnerable citizens are less likely to be abandoned in difficult times.

In Liverpool, the City Council can take credit for its foresight two decades ago, when in the late 1990s it established a Community Based Economic Development Unit. This Unit was instrumental in accelerating the development of a series of successful community business among which the Furniture Resource Centre, the Alt Valley Trust, Lister Steps, Crawford House, and Blackburne House were notable examples.

The Alt Valley Trust began working in 1983 in in Croxteth on the outskirts of Liverpool, in what was then the largest housing estate in Europe, and which had been long afflicted by unemployment, crime, and low aspiration. Local people, furious at plans to close down their local secondary school, occupied the building and for three years ran the school themselves, until the council decided to restore funding. The Trust then took over a disused old people's home and declared that they would create a 'Communiversity' for Croxteth. They went on to establish apprenticeships in construction and other trades, and launched a series of community businesses, bringing a failing leisure centre into community management, and taking over a local pub, and much else besides. It was, and remains, a striking example of what local people are capable of in the most adverse circumstances.

Blackburne House occupies a former girls' school in the famous Hope Street quarter of the city. This listed building had lain empty for eight years, until in 1994 the community business raised £4m for refurbishment, creating a beautiful and inspiring venue for education and training. It ran a series of community businesses: a cafe, nursery, construction company, conference centre, and graphic design company, applying surpluses to support the building of skills among the hardest to reach and disadvantaged women in the city. As its Chief Executive Claire Dove, who also became Chair of Social Enterprise UK, says 'We are driven by our values, which are embedded into all we do. We want women to be inspired by their educational experience with us and to realise economic independence once they start their chosen careers.'

In places like Liverpool it seemed that success followed success: once a handful of community businesses were up and running and demonstrating what was possible word spread quickly and others were inspired to have a go, with or without council support. And some were to achieve national and even international renown. In 2011 the Granby Four Streets community land trust was formed to renovate a group of four streets in a Liverpool neighbourhood which has the oldest Black community in Britain, but which had suffered from long term deprivation and which from the 1970s had become increasingly derelict. The community business took a creative approach to refurbishing the empty homes and brightening up the neighbourhood, and supported by architecture and design collective Assemble, the scheme won the 2015 Turner Prize.

Homebaked is a community bakery in Anfield, selling 1,200 pies a week to the crowds of football supporters who flock past on match days to nearby Liverpool Football Club. It also provides a welcoming meeting place for the neighbourhood, not least through its popular cake club. With grant support from Power to Change it is refurbishing the flat above the bakery, to rent it at an affordable rate to local young people, including trainees who will contribute to the building work on the flat, and has set up a community land trust to extend this approach to nearby derelict buildings. In effect Homebaked is reviving the early co-operative model of generating surpluses through a shop in order to create a better community, 'rebuilding the neighbourhood brick by brick and loaf by loaf'.

Liverpool is not the only city which had the foresight and vision to invest in its local community businesses. In the mid-1990s Sheffield City Council created the Sheffield Community Economic Development Unit, which continued to operate until 2012, and there were similar sustained efforts by local authorities elsewhere, not least in Bristol and Bradford. In more rural districts, such as Northumberland and Calderdale, the local authority also played a prominent role over many years. Their efforts helped to build a critical mass of community business activity, creating the conditions for community activists to share their experience and their expertise, and build local networks of mutual support, collaboration, and trade. Today the results are evident, as it is often in these areas that the community business movement is most advanced.

The upsurge of the community business movement in recent years, despite the adverse climate of austerity in which it has had to operate, is a phenomenon unprecedented in the long history of community business.

A number of circumstances have come together to make this possible. The willingness of local and national government, albeit rarely in a sufficiently sustained way, to promote and support community business, right across traditional party political fault lines, has been a historically recent phenomenon, as has been the provision of significant public, trust, and lottery funding dedicated to community business. As we have seen, concerted efforts, however imperfect, have taken place to build an evidence base and to tell a more compelling and convincing story of the impact of community business. The big increase in asset ownership has enabled many community businesses to build up a strong balance sheet, and provided always that the assets are not encumbered with liabilities and restrictions, this has proved time and again the surest protection against the inevitable setbacks and shocks which every community business will encounter.

Above all we have seen in recent years increasingly vigorous networks of community businesses, formed by community businesses themselves, at both national and local levels. This has made it much easier for skills and experience to be shared, encouraging trust and generous leadership, and stimulating all participants to raise their game. In these peer networks, success has been celebrated and failure has been minimised, and where failure has occurred, it has been learned from, and time and again has become a springboard for future ventures.

Afterword

What might
the future hold?

**The story of community business, stretching back many
hundreds of years, helps us to realise that the strength and
endurance of the community business movement is not simply
about breadth and scale in the here and now, but that we also
have depth and scale in the past.**

As to the future, there are some things we can be reasonably sure
of. Some of the causes of failure in the past are less prevalent for
community businesses today; for example, the lack of suitable
legal forms within which a community business can operate is
no longer a significant barrier. Access to sufficient quantities
of suitable finance will always be a challenge, but the range of
options available has widened significantly and hopefully that will
continue.

One thing is certain: community business will never become easy.
Leaders of community businesses no longer face the prospect
of imprisonment for seditious activities, but it is by no means
uncommon for successful and high profile community business
today to experience hostile scrutiny, often in an intense and
highly personalised form. This is perhaps not surprising. After all,
community businesses pose a challenge at the most fundamental
level to the accepted ways of delivering public services, of meeting
the challenges of impoverished communities, and of running
businesses. The more successful they become, the more they can

attract opposition from institutional vested interests.

Yet, at the same time the story of community business over the centuries suggests that it will continue to attract enthusiastic support from unlikely places, from radicals and conservatives, from the very poorest in society and from the very richest.

Our history can help us understand that crude attempts to co-opt community business as a cheaper alternative to public service delivery, while imposing on community business a public sector regime of standardisation, compliance and risk aversion, will inevitably fail. The vital and distinctive strengths of community business, whether arising from mutual aid, or philanthropy, or radical systems change, or a combination of these, all run in the opposite direction.

Our history can also help us predict and hopefully resist the inevitable attempts to commercialise, regulate and professionalise those types of community business which become, by virtue of their trading success, attractive for private investors, as happened with most building societies and many housing associations.

There are other dangers ahead. We have seen in the past how a small number of high profile failures can discredit a whole movement, as happened at various stages in the co-operative movement, and in the community business movement in Scotland in the early 1990s. But we have also seen how community businesses have regrouped and recovered, always building fresh momentum.

Our history gives us hope that, however difficult the journey, and however many obstacles line the path, it will be possible to grow an ever more resilient movement, capable of endurance, creating the conditions whereby community businesses could operate in a successful and sustained way in any neighbourhood anywhere in the country.

Will community business become the favoured vehicle of the

wealthy and powerful in society to realise their philanthropic goals? Will it become the means by which ordinary people will combine, through mutual aid, to take back control? Will it become a principal driver for social change and social justice in our communities? We have found evidence of all of this in the past, and we may see much more in the future.

Most significantly, today we are seeing profound change all around us at a pace never before experienced, not even during the early industrial revolution, nor in the period in which the welfare state was created. Demographic change, climate change, technological change, change in the patterns of work and leisure and the movement of peoples, all of these will have a transformative impact on community life, generating new possibilities, creating new tensions, benefiting some but leaving others catastrophically behind. No doubt we will also see the rise of radically new types of association and organisational form. One thing is sure therefore, that in the future community businesses will look different, take on new causes, and undertake activities which today we can hardly imagine.

And yet, if our history tells us anything it tells us that despite all change, the core impulse of community business, trading for good, remains valid and irrepressible. Today the community business movement seems poised to step into the future with confidence, with eyes wide open, ready to anticipate the trials and tribulations ahead, willing to challenge itself and rise to the occasion. If it is indeed able to do so, it will play a part in creating resilient and responsive communities, in every part of the country, on the front foot and ready for anything the future might hold.

Acknowledgements

I would like to thank Vidhya Alakeson at Power to Change for commissioning this history, her colleagues Mark Gordon and Charlotte Whittaker who acted as my editors with patience, insight and considerable skill, and Ged Devlin, Gen Maitland Hudson and Richard Harries for their helpful advice. Caroline Macfarland from Common Vision brought creative flair and sound judgment, and my thanks to Caroline and her colleagues for all their work on the design and the final drafts. Ed Mayo from Co-ops UK recommended me for the task – thank you Ed, I've enjoyed it immensely. Thanks also to Peter Couchman, formerly at the Plunkett Foundation, who always shared my enthusiasm for the subject and to James Alcock who told me about Tafarn Y Fic, the first co-operative community pub. Thank you Jess Steele for introducing me to the America Ground in Hastings and for inspiring us all with her prodigious energy for community business.

I have learned much, not least about stokvel, pardner and other lending circles, from Yvonne Field from the Ubele initiative, which promotes entrepreneurial social action within African diaspora communities. Robin Grey shares my belief that radical movements flourish according to the stories they can tell, and also in his case, the songs they can sing. The chapter on community business in Scotland owes a great deal to the knowledge and generosity of Alan Kay, Simon Teasdale, Gillian Murray and Les Huckfield at the Yunus Centre for Social Business and Health, as well as Carole McCallum, University Archivist at Glasgow Caledonian University. I had the privilege of access to collections at the British Library, and my warm thanks to all the staff there. I am forever grateful to the late Professor Yasuo Nishiyama from Tokyo University who first kindled my interest in the history of our movement on one of his many visits to the UK, and I want to thank my former colleagues and friends at the Development Trusts Association and Locality, especially Hugh Rolo, among whom I have learned much of what I know about community business in modern times. Above all I want to thank the multitude of practitioners, past and present, who have been sometimes bloody-minded, often brilliant, and always brave in their pursuit of community business and have created a history which needed to be told – I know I have not done you justice, but I hope I have at least made a start.

Select bibliography

I owe a particular debt to two excellent accounts of utopian experiments in Britain: Heavens Below: Utopian Experiments in England 1560-1960, by W H G Armytage, 1961, and Utopia Britannica: British Utopian Experiments 1325 – 1945, by Chris Coates, 2001. I have also drawn on material from my earlier publication A History of Community Asset Ownership, published by the Development Trusts Association (now Locality) with the Joseph Rowntree Foundation in 2009.

1. Community confraternities

Wage Labour and Guilds in Medieval Europe, Steven A Epstein, 1991.

Women in Medieval Guilds, Robert Ferrell, 1999.

The Art of Solidarity in the Middle Ages: Guilds in England 1250-1550, Gervase Rosser, 2015.

Heaven and Earth in Anglo-Saxon England: Theology and Society in an Age of Faith, Helen Foxhall Forbes, 2013.

Guild Solidarity and Charity in Florence, Ghent and London, c. 1300-1550, Arie van Steensel, 2016.

2. From guilds to friendly societies

British Friendly Societies, 1750–1914, Simon Cordery, 2003.

British Clubs and Societies 1580-1800: The Origins of an Associational World, Peter Clark, 2000.

The Needs of Strangers: Friendly Societies and Insurance Societies in Late Eighteenth-Century England, Elizabeth Kowaleski Wallace, 2000.

The Friendly Societies in England, 1815-1875, P H J H Gosden, 1961.

Supporting self-help: charity, mutuality and reciprocity in nineteenth-century, Daniel Britain, in: Bridgen, Paul and Bernard, Harris eds. Charity and Mutual Aid in Europe and North America since 1800, 2007.

Reinventing Civil Society, David Green, 1993.

3. A vision of utopia

A Fruteful and a Pleasaunt Worke of the Beste State of a Publique Weal and of the New Ile called Utopia, Sir Thomas More, first edition in English 1551, originally published in Latin in 1516.

4. Little commonwealths

The Law of Freedom in a Platform or True Magistracy Restored, Gerrard Winstanley, 1652.

The World Turned Upside Down, Christopher Hill, 1975.

Levellers in the English Revolution, G E Aylmer, 1975.

The Pursuit of the Millennium: Revolutionary millenarians and mystical anarchists of the Middle Ages, Norman Cohn, 1957.

5. The early Quakers and plans for a college of industry

Proposals for Raising a College of Industry of All Useful Trades and Husbandry, John Bellers, 1695.

Two Centuries of Industrial Welfare: the London (Quaker) Lead Company, Arthur Raistrick, 1988.

Dreamstreets: A Journey Through Britain's Village Utopias, Jacqueline Yallop, 2016.

6. For the benefit of the congregation

A History of the Moravian Church, J E Hutton, 1909.

The Application of Associative Principles and Methods to Agriculture, Charles Kingsley, 1851.

A Yorkshire Source of Decorated Paper in the Eighteenth Century, Tanya Schmoller, 2003.

The Second Coming, Popular Milleniarianism 1780-1850, JFC Harrison, 1979.

7. Not mere spectators in the world

The Political Works of Thomas Spence, H T Dickinson, 1982.

The Life and Times of Thomas Spence, P M Ashraf, 1983.

Thomas Spence: the Poor Man's Revolutionary, ed Alastair Bennett, Keith Armstrong, 2014.

8. Milling and mutual aid

Co-operative Corn Milling: Self-help during the grain crises of the Napoleonic Wars, Jennifer Tann, 1980.

Consumer-owned community flour and bread societies in the eighteenth and early 19th centuries, Joshua Bamfield, in The Emergence of Modern Retailing 1750-1950, ed N S Alexander, 1998.

The Moral Economy of the English Crowd in the Eighteenth Century, E P Thompson, 1971.

9. A new moral world

Adventures in Socialism: New Lanark establishment and Orbiston community, Alex Cullen, 1910.

Co-operation and the Owenite socialist communities in Britain 1825-1845, R G Garnett, 1972.

Robert Owen and the Owenites in Britain and America: the Quest for the New Moral World, J F C Harrison, 1969.

10. A common interest and a common tie

The History of Co-operation, George Jacob Holyoake, 1906.

Through sixty years: A record of progress and achievement, Ipswich Industrial and Co-operative Society Limited, W H Adsett, 1928

11. Fustian jackets, blistered hands and unshorn chins

The Chartist Land Company, Alice Mary Hadfield, 1970, reprinted 2000.

A Practical Work on the Management of Small Farms, Feargus O'Connor, 1843.

The Making of the English Working Class, E P Thompson, 1963, revised ed 1968.

12. Building societies

Common Ground – for Mutual Home Ownership, Pat Conaty, Johnston Birchall, Steve Bendle, and Rosemary Foggitt, 2003.

13. Model communities

Enlightened Entrepreneurs, Ian Campbell Bradley, 1987.

Salt and Silver: a story of hope, Jim Greenhalf, 1998.

One Man's Vision: The Story of the Joseph Rowntree Village Trust, L E Waddilove, 1954.

14. Darkest England and the way out

Hadleigh Salvation Army Farm: A vision reborn, Gordon Parkhill, Graham Cook, 2018, revised 2015.

Alternative Communities in 19th Century England, Dennis Hardy, 1979.

Community Experiments 1900-1945, Dennis Hardy, 2000.

15. In Times of Trouble

The Brynmawr Furniture Makers: a Quaker initiative, 1929-1940, Mary, Eurwyn, Dafydd Wiliam, 2012.

16. Place making: there is another way

Taking on the Motorway: North Kensington Amenity Trust 21 Years, Andrew Duncan, 1992.

Fabulous Beasts: Stories of Community Enterprise from the DTA, ed. Henry Palmer, 2002.

17. Immigration and Enterprise

Strangers, Aliens and Asians: Huguenots, Jews and Bangladeshis in Spitalfields 1660 -2000, Anne Kershen, 2005.

The Chinese in Britain 1800 to the Present: Economy, Transnationalism, Identity, Gregor Benton and Edmund Terence Gomez, 2008.

Kate Murray, 'Black housing bodies helped build communities.' Article in The Guardian newspaper, 8 Dec 2010.

Deep Roots, Diverse Communities, Dedicated Service: The legacy, value and future potential of Black and Minority Ethnic housing organisations in England, Kevin Gulliver and Dawn Prentice, 2016.

Social enterprise and ethnic minorities, Leandro Sepulveda, Stephen Syrett and Sara Calvo, Third Sector Research Centre, 2010.

18. A voyage significant and hazardous

Nothing without work – Govan Workspace, Pat Cassidy, in: The First Ten Years: A decade of Community Enterprise in Scotland, Community Business Scotland, 1987. *[SECS-SECS/JP/2/2/1/2/048]

Community Business and the Intermediate Labour Market: the West of Scotland experience, Simon Clark and Alan McGregor, 1997. *[SECS-SECS/JP/2/2/1/2/038]

Community Business Scotland, 1986 Directory.

Community Business in Scotland, K Hayton, I Turok, J Gordon and J Gray, 1993.

A critical examination of the role of community business in urban regeneration, in: Town Planning Review, Vol 67:1: 1-20, Keith Hayton, 1996.

Reflections on Barrowfield Community Business Ltd, Report to Strathclyde Community Business Ltd, Andrew A McArthur, 1990. *[SECS-SECS/JP/2/2/1/2/019]

Communities at Work: the contribution of community businesses, Glasgow University, Alan McGregor and Andrew McArthur, 1988.

Community Enterprise: What is it? In: The First Ten Years: A decade of Community Enterprise in Scotland, Community Business Scotland, John Pearce, 1987.

Learning from Failure: Lessons in how to strengthen and build the social enterprise sector. John Pearce, 2005.

Strathclyde Community Business, Annual reports 1984/85, 1985/86, 1986/87. *[SECS-SECS/JP/2/2/1/2/005, SECS-SECS/JP/2/2/1/2/007, SECS-SECS/JP/2/2/1/2/009]

An evaluation of community business in Scotland, Alan McGregor, 1988 *[SECS-SECS/JP/2/2/1/2/012]

(*These publications are available at the Glasgow Caledonian University Archive Centre: John Pearce Collection; archive references in brackets).

19. All right then, why don't you buy it yourselves?

A History of Preston in Hertfordshire, The Red Lion in the 1980s, Philip Wray, 2015, sourced from http://www.prestonherts.co.uk/page181.html.

Co-operative Pubs: A better form of business, Plunkett Foundation, 2014.

Friends on Tap: The role of pubs at the heart of the community, Professor Robin Dunbar, 2016.

20. We've become trendy

The New History of the C.W.S, Percy Redfern, 1938.

Building Co-operation: A business history of The Co-operative Group, J F Wilson, A Webster and R Vorberg-Rugh, 2013.

Community Shops: A better form of business, Plunkett Foundation, 2014.

21. To have and to hold

From the Low Tide of the Sea to the Highest Mountain Tops: Community ownership of land in the Highlands and Islands of Scotland, James Hunter, 2012.

To Have and to Hold: The Development Trusts Association guide to asset development for community and social enterprises, second edition, Lorraine Hart, 2010.

Annual Membership Survey, Development Trusts Association, 2012.

Community Land Trust Handbook, ed. Catherine Harrington and Rose Seagrief, 2012.

Understanding the Potential of Small Scale Community Led Housing, Locality, Jo Gooding and Tom Johnston, 2015.

22. Community rights

Making Assets Work: The Quirk Review of community management and ownership of public assets, 2007.

Community ownership and management of assets, Joseph Rowntree Foundation, Mike Aiken, Ben Cairns, Stephen Thake, 2008.

Whose Society? The Final Big Society Audit, Civil Exchange, 2015.

Information about community rights at: http://mycommunity.org.uk/

Community managed libraries: good practice toolkit and case studies at: https://www.gov.uk/government/collections/community-libraries-good-practice-toolkit

23. Investing for good

Sustainable futures: investing in community-based organisations, Stephen Thake, 2004.

Responsible Finance: The industry in 2016, Theodora Hadjimichael and John McLean, 2017. How to make the most of community shares, Community Shares Unit, 2016.

How to Measure and Report Social Impact: A guide for investees, The Social Investment Business Group, 2014.

The Money Trail: Measuring your impact on the local economy using LM3, New Economics Foundation, 2002.

Measuring social wealth: a study of social audit practice for community and co-operative enterprises, John Pearce, 1996 [Glasgow Caledonian University Archive Centre: John Pearce Collection – archive reference 658.408 P21].

Hill Holt Wood: Social Accounts, 2005.

Measuring Social Value, Claudia Wood and Daniel Leighton, 2010.

Getting Started in Social Impact Measurement: A guide to choosing how to measure social impact, Helene Rinaldo, 2010.

24. Against all the odds

Locality Membership: A snapshot, Locality, 2016.

Community Business Market in 2016, Doug Hull, Tom Davies and Adam Swersky, Social Finance for Power to Change, 2016.

Index

About the author

Steve Wyler is an independent consultant and writer in the social sector. From 2000 to 2014 Steve was Chief Executive of Locality and (previously) the Development Trusts Association, building a network of community businesses dedicated to community enterprise, community ownership, and social change. Steve has been a member of Government advisory groups on localism, social enterprise, and the third sector. Steve also helped to establish Social Enterprise UK and the Adventure Capital Fund (parent body of the Social Investment Business). He was awarded an OBE in the 2011 New Year Honours List.

About Power to Change

Power to Change is an independent charitable trust set up in 2015 to grow community business across England.

No one understands a community better than the people who live there. Power to Change works with community businesses to revive local assets, protect the services people rely on, and address local needs.

We have an endowment from the Big Lottery Fund which we will use to strengthen community businesses by providing money, advice and support to help local people come together to take control. At a time when many parts of the country face cuts, neglect and social problems, we want to make sure local areas survive and stay vibrant.